A Political Adventure Filled with Stories,
Photos, Speeches, Cartoons, and Trivia

Republican's

Soul

What It Means to Be Γ

D1055768

Health Communications, Inc.
Deerfield Beach, Florida

www.hcibooks.com

The views and opinions expressed in *Republican's Soul* are those of the contributors and do not necessarily reflect the views and opinions of Health Communications, Inc., or its employees.

Library of Congress Cataloging-in-Publication Data
is available from the Library of Congress.

Publisher: Health Communications, Inc.
 3201 S.W. 15th Street
 Deerfield Beach, FL 33442-8190

All speeches reprinted in this book are from www.americanrhetoric.com

Edited by Andrea Gold
Trivia, pages 10, 38, 66, 90, 142 by Dan Murphy
Cover photo © Fotolia.com
Cover design by Larissa Hise Henoch
Interior design and formatting by Lawna Patterson Oldfield
Photos pages 9, 37, 141 © Getty Images
Photo page 65 © Gary Keefer/AFP/Getty Images
Photos pages 89, 111, and 167 © AFP/Getty Images

Contents

Introduction

Politics. The word alone evokes a vast array of emotions. In the context of our lives, politics conjures up imagery, memories, opinions, and heated debates, and the word "politics"—in and of itself—can't help but be extremely personal.

For many, making a party affiliation (no matter the party) can be one of the most defining and memorable moments of one's life. Your own political beliefs are a testament to your character, igniting your passions, strengthening your convictions, and exemplifying what you hold most dear and true in your heart. In *Republican's Soul*, we set out on a journey to explore the personal significance that being a Republican has on one's own history, development, ideologies, relationships, and so much more.

Republican's Soul is not only an exploration, but a commemoration of the nostalgia and pride each party member has for its founders, its fighters, and its future. And what you'll find throughout these pages encapsulates good old Republican zeal with compelling first-person stories from fellow Republicans, wit and wisdom from some of your favorite leaders, historical tidbits, and photos that illustrate the pivotal moments in Republican history. Along the way, you'll laugh at clever cartoons, reminisce while reading excerpts from inspiring Republican speeches, and test your political knowledge with trivia and must-know facts.

All in all, this political pick-me-up will entertain, educate, and inspire you about what it means to be a part of the GOP.

Republican
Presidential Time Line

Abraham Lincoln		1861–1865 *and* 1865	*Republican*
Ulysses S. Grant		1869–1873 *and* 1873–1877	*Republican*
Rutherford B. Hayes		1877–1881	*Republican*
James Garfield		1881–1881	*Republican*
Chester A. Arthur		1881–1885	*Republican*
Benjamin Harrison		1889–1893	*Republican*
William McKinley		1897–1901	*Republican*
Theodore Roosevelt		1901–1905 *and* 1905–1909	*Republican*

William H. Taft 1909–1913 *Republican*

Warren G. Harding 1921–1923 *Republican*

Calvin Coolidge 1923–1925 *and* 1925–1929 *Republican*

Herbert C. Hoover 1929–1933 *Republican*

Dwight D. Eisenhower 1953–1961 *Republican*

Richard M. Nixon 1969–1973 *and* 1973–1974 *Republican*

Gerald R. Ford 1974–1977 *Republican*

Ronald W. Reagan 1981–1985 *and* 1985–1989 *Republican*

George Herbert Walker Bush 1989–1993 *Republican*

George Walker Bush 2001–present *Republican*

Secret Lives of Men

As a child in Philadelphia, I discussed politics around the kitchen table with my dad the way other dads and sons talked sports. The only thing I could tell you about Philadelphia sports was that by the time the first pitch was thrown on opening day, the Phillies were already statistically eliminated from playoff contention.

Philadelphia was a pure Democrat town. Everyone was a Democrat. In fact, Philadelphians once voted for a dead Democrat over a live Republican. My mom is still a far-left Democrat, trying to figure out where she went wrong with me. I recall how upset she was when she found "that" magazine in my room. No, not *Playboy* . . . the *National Review*.

When I was a child and walked into the voting booth with my dad and watched him vote for Richard Nixon, I was shocked. I turned to him and said, "Dad, you voted for Nixon. He's a Republican."

"Yes, he is, and don't tell your mother," he responded.

I kept that secret until my dad passed away.

I was a Democrat for years until I started working. I would study my paycheck and try to figure out who the FICA family was and wonder why I was sending so much money to them every week. Around that time, I became a Republican.

Years later when my girlfriend, now my wife, wanted me to meet her folks, I was excited until she told me I could not discuss politics with them. I was to meet Heidi's mom and dad, but I was forbidden to talk politics—period!

Heidi introduced me to her mom and then quickly sat me with her father. It took me all of about thirty seconds to exhaust my knowledge of baseball and golf (the subjects Heidi told me to discuss with him), and then we started talking politics. I realized that we were actually agreeing on everything. At this point I leaned in close and whispered, "You are a Republican, aren't you?"

He leaned in even closer and said, "Yes, but don't tell Heidi's mom." I felt right at home!

Jeff Katz

What a Hero Looks Like

Hurrying to the airport in his limousine, Joe Foss, Republican governor of South Dakota, pulled to a hard stop when he saw a nine-year-old newspaper boy take a fall from his bicycle in the middle of the highway. I was that boy.

Balancing fifty to a hundred newspapers on a bike was a challenge, and when I hit a rut, I crashed onto the pavement and newspapers scattered across the highway. I looked up to see a black limousine fast approaching and coming straight at me. Heart racing, scared and embarrassed, I scrambled to get out of harm's way. As the limousine screeched to a halt, I spotted the license plate with the number "1"— immediately I knew this was the official limousine of the South Dakota governor.

To my amazement, Governor Joe Foss pulled to the side of the road, stepped out of the limousine, and, dressed in a business suit, started picking up newspapers.

I knew little about this man or his political views. I did not know Joe Foss had been a Wildcat fighter pilot in World War II, leading a band of fearless pilots who became known as "Joe's Flying Circus," shooting down seventy-two planes in the fight for Guadalcanal. I did not know Joe was a national hero with twenty-six personal aerial victories against the Japanese—equaling the record set by Eddie Rickenbacker in World War I. I did not know Joe Foss had been shot down in the waters off Malaita Island, went under with his plane, gulped salt water, nearly drowned before freeing himself, and then fought off sharks before being rescued. I did not know Joe Foss had received the Bronze Star, the Silver Star, the Purple Heart; nor did I know that President Franklin Roosevelt had presented Joe with the highest award for valor in military action, the Congressional Medal of Honor. I did not know he lived out his faith in the public arena as governor and later as the first commissioner of the American Football League.

Another thing I did not know about Joe Foss was that in 1941, he was the Officer of the Day, in charge of base security at Pensacola, when the Japanese attacked Pearl Harbor. Joe Foss rode around the perimeter of this strategic air base, defending against would-be Japanese invaders, utilizing the only transportation available . . . a bicycle.

Was this on his mind as he saw me take a bicycle spill in the middle of the airport highway? When Joe Foss offered, "Let me help pick up your papers," and began chasing newspapers scattered across the road, I was in awe. Without fanfare—no cheering crowds, no medals, and no bands playing on the highway to the airport—Joe, the governor with a state to manage and a plane to catch, took a few minutes to help a kid with a skinned knee. A politician par excellence—may God increase their numbers.

True greatness. Joe was my hero.

Dave Beckwith

Reprinted by permission of Atlantic Feature Syndicate. ©1995 Atlantic Feature Syndicate.

WHO SAID IT?

No person was ever honored for what he received. Honor has been the reward for what he gave.

—*Calvin Coolidge*

America is never wholly herself unless she is engaged in high moral principle. We as a people have such a purpose today. It is to make kinder the face of the nation and gentler the face of the world.

—*George H. W. Bush*

Unlike any other nation, here the people rule, and their will is the supreme law. It is sometimes sneeringly said by those who do not like free government, that here we count heads. True, heads are counted, but brains also . . .

—*William McKinley*

Better to remain silent and be thought a fool than to speak out and remove all doubt.

—*Abraham Lincoln*

My country owes me nothing.
It gave me, as it gives every boy and girl,
a chance. It gave me schooling, independence of
action, opportunity for service and honor.
In no other land could a boy from a country
village, without inheritance or influential friends,
look forward with unbounded hope.

—*Herbert Hoover*

Keep your eyes
on the stars and your
feet on the ground.

—*Theodore Roosevelt*

There is nothing wrong
with America that the faith, love of
freedom, intelligence, and energy
of her citizens cannot cure.

—*Dwight D. Eisenhower*

We are a nation that
has a government—not the
other way around. And that
makes us special among the
nations of the earth.

—*Ronald Reagan*

President Abraham Lincoln
Gettysburg Address
Delivered November 19, 1863

Fourscore and seven years ago our fathers brought forth on this continent a new nation, conceived in liberty and dedicated to the proposition that all men are created equal.

Now we are engaged in a great civil war, testing whether that nation or any nation so conceived and so dedicated can long endure. We are met on a great battlefield of that war. We have come to dedicate a portion of that field as a final resting-place for those who here gave their lives that that nation might live. It is altogether fitting and proper that we should do this.

But, in a larger sense, we cannot dedicate, we cannot consecrate, we cannot hallow this ground. The brave men, living and dead who struggled here have consecrated it far above our poor power to add or detract. The world will little note nor long remember what we say here, but it can never forget what they did here. It is for us the living rather to be dedicated here to the unfinished work which they who fought here have thus far so nobly advanced. It is rather for us to be here dedicated to the great task remaining before us—that from these honored dead we take increased devotion to that cause for which they gave the last full measure of devotion—that we here highly resolve that these dead shall not have died in vain, that this nation under God shall have a new birth of freedom, and that government of the people, by the people, for the people shall not perish from the earth.

A great moment in Republican history: November 19, 1863—President Abraham Lincoln delivers The Gettysburg Address at the dedication of the Soldiers' National Cemetery in Gettysburg, Pennsylvania.

1. Which Republican presidents are on Mount Rushmore?

2. Who was the first Republican presidential candidate?

3. Who was the only president to serve without being elected?

4. Who were the only vice presidents to serve without being elected?

5. Who was the first African American to serve in Congress?

6. Who was the first woman elected to Congress?

7. Which Republicans won the presidency while losing the popular vote?

8. Where and when was the Republican Party born?

9. Who was the only Republican to serve as Speaker of the House between 1931 and 1994?

10. Who served the shortest term as Speaker of the House?

11. Who was the only president to serve as Chief Justice?

1. Abraham Lincoln and Theodore Roosevelt

2. John C. Fremont, "The Pathfinder," in 1856

3. Gerald R. Ford, 1974–1977

4. Gerald R. Ford, 1973–1974 and Nelson Rockefeller, 1974–1977

5. Hiram Rhodes Revels of Mississippi was elected to fill the last year of an unexpired term in the United States Senate. He served in the Senate 1870–1871.

6. Jeannette Rankin of Montana was elected to the House of Representatives in 1916. She ran unsuccessfully for the Senate in 1918 as an Independent. She won reelection to the House in 1940. She voted against American intervention in World War I in 1917. She was the only person to vote against entering World War II in 1941.

7. Rutherford B. Hayes in 1876, Benjamin Harrison in 1888, George W. Bush in 2000

8. Ripon, Wisconsin, on March 20, 1854, founded by a group of citizens opposed to the Kansas-Nebraska Act and the possible extension of slavery into the western territories

9. Joseph William Martin, Jr. of Massachusetts, Speaker 1947–1949 and 1953–1955

10. Theodore Medad Pomeroy of New York, Speaker March 3, 1869

11. William Howard Taft, President 1909–1913, Chief Justice 1921–1930

Tales of a Mixed Marriage

It was 1957. I was nineteen years old and living in Brooklyn, New York. I had fallen in love with a tall, handsome, twenty-four-year-old engineer from Queens. Ed and I had been dating for close to a year, and although we were ready for a permanent commitment, we knew we would have to wait. Conscription—mandatory military service—was still in effect that year, and Ed was due to be drafted.

Two months after we met, Ed and I realized we were different religions. After much discussion, we agreed we could overcome this obstacle with respect and understanding.

One night, Ed arrived to pick me up for our date wearing his I LIKE IKE button. I watched my mother's knees buckle, but she quickly regained her balance. My father just sighed and rolled his eyes. The rest of the family looked as if they had been turned to stone, but, thankfully, no one screamed or fainted. I was so proud of my blue-collar, staunchly Democratic family that night. I decided to tackle this new problem later, went out on our date, and had a great time.

The next morning, my family gathered around to offer their condolences and ask me what I was going to do. I assured them that I knew love could conquer all and that I still intended to accept Ed's proposal, if it came. At an opportune moment, I told Ed about my family's political affiliations. He just laughed and promised not to wear his I LIKE IKE button the next time he picked me up. We agreed that fate seemed to be conspiring against us, but we felt love and a great sense of humor were all we needed.

Ed was drafted that year, much to my parents' relief. They really liked Ed, but they felt that with him out of the picture, I might find a nice Catholic Democrat to marry.

Both our families had concerns about our marrying, but Ed and I knew we had something worth fighting for. We decided not to let their doubts jeopardize our relationship. So, despite the reelection of Dwight D. Eisenhower, we became engaged after Ed's tour of duty. In September 1959, this Irish-Catholic Democrat married her wonderful German-Protestant Republican.

Ed and I lived in a two-family house with his mother and his older brother and his family while we were looking for a house. Ed's family were and still are dedicated Republicans. I knew they hadn't been too happy about my religion, but I never asked how they reacted to my politics. I guess the subject never came up because that year, when I turned twenty-one and registered to vote as a Democrat, they were shocked.

One afternoon, Ed's brother brought in the mail and reluctantly handed me a letter from the New York State Democratic Committee. "This is the first piece of Democratic mail ever to be delivered to this house," he solemnly announced. That day, I realized that both of our families were dealing with a revolutionary concept. At that point, Ed and I vowed never to discuss religion or politics with either family. I promised to wear my KENNEDY FOR PRESIDENT button only when visiting my folks.

Over the years, many lively political discussions have been held at our kitchen table, with Ed coming down in favor of big business and me championing more programs for the poor. I must confess that I have, on occasion, voted for a Republican and Ed for a Democrat.

One day, soon after our oldest daughter began working, she was having lunch with friends from her office. One of them asked, "Paula, who are your parents voting for in the upcoming election?" She responded, "My dad is voting for George Bush, and my mom is voting for Bill Clinton." Her friends were shocked. "You must be mistaken, Paula. Wives don't vote for different candidates than their husbands." Being the product of a "mixed marriage," I found this remark quite funny. "Maybe in your family they don't, but in my family, my parents often vote for opposing candidates. Besides, you obviously don't know my mom very well, do you?"

In 2000, I was watching the Democratic convention when new friends of ours dropped by for a visit. "You're watching the Democratic convention?" one of them asked in horror. "Of course," I answered. "We watch both conventions. How do you know what each party stands for if you don't watch both conventions? Besides, Ed's the Republican in this family. I'm a Democrat." Over the years, Ed and I have enjoyed watching our friends' reactions when we reveal that we are from opposite sides of the aisle. Our new friends just looked confused.

In recent years, our political beliefs have become more alike. We both want this terrible war to end; we worry about the talk of overturning *Roe* v. *Wade*; and we believe that outsourcing jobs has had a disastrous effect on our economy. We fear that government has begun to assume the role of religion: embracing all the taboos and restrictions, but not the virtues of charity and compassion.

In September 2009, Ed and I will have been married fifty years.

Life certainly has been exciting and interesting. We raised four wonderful children who watch both parties' political conventions and are far more open-minded than their parents' families. I believe we are living proof that Donkeys and Elephants can coexist, even in the institution of marriage. I guess the moral is that with enough love and a heavy dose of humor, you truly can live happily ever after.

Barbara Ann Carle

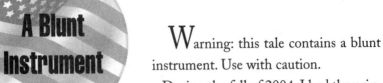

A Blunt Instrument

Warning: this tale contains a blunt instrument. Use with caution.

During the fall of 2004, I had the privilege of teaching an intense college class called *Political Communication*. In the course, the students learned about communicating in and through the political process by participating in it in a variety of ways. One of these ways was by registering others to vote. No one in the class, including myself, had ever been deputized to register others to vote. So, together we took our oath and began canvassing our community. My students were inspiring. Vanessa decided that she would register all of the university's student athletes. By the last day, she had registered 90 percent of them. Migdalia decided that she would focus on the housekeeping and physical plant staffs. She convinced the head of this division to call a meeting of all these employees just so they could register. Nichol, the daughter of two confirmed nonvoters, went home, registered her parents, and took them to vote in November.

Of course, asking people if they are registered to vote can lead to some challenging conversations: sometimes confusing, sometimes contentious. Some students confused registering to vote with registering for the Selective Service. Some out-of-town students were confused about where they could vote, surprised that they had to vote in the precinct in the county in which they were registered. However, these confusing situations were easily cleared up. The real challenge emerged when we came up against citizens who sneered at us saying, "Why should I register to vote? Why should I care about politics? Why bother? Government stuff is irrelevant to me." As a class, we discussed different ways to counter these disdainful responses and turn the encounter into a positive experience, resulting in the disdainful person ultimately registering to vote. We reminded disdainful students about the importance of federal and state financial aid in their collegiate lives. We reminded those who snorted that the government and the civic process were irrelevant that the government did things like build roads, provide Social Security, and inspect meat and milk. Nevertheless, despite trying to connect these potential voters with civic realities in their lives, some of these encounters turned out badly, with student registrars being yelled at or being treated in an ugly manner.

One late afternoon, before our weekly *Political Communication* class meeting, I was sitting restlessly in my campus office. As I was mulling over how we could handle these situations in a more positive way, my husband popped in with a hot-off-the-press copy of *The 9-11 Commission Report: Final Report of the National Commission on Terrorist Attacks Upon the United States*. Frustrated with my class planning, I cracked open this anxiously awaited government report, fascinated with its excruciating detail of that fateful day. After reading for about twenty minutes, I stumbled over a couple of lines that knocked the wind out of me. Here, in the pages of this horrifying report, I suddenly found the answer to our class's registration dilemma. Here in the pages of this horrifying report was *the* reason to vote. Quickly, I typed in those few lines of the report into my computer in a large bold font, ran the counter up to 100, and hit print.

Our class gathered that evening in good spirits as we talked excitedly about the first Debate Watch program, sponsored by the Commission on Presidential Debates, that we would soon be hosting. Eventually, the discussion came around to the contentious conversations we had all experienced with a few of our fellow citizens. Danny, the liberal, and Danny, the conservative, offered that by working together they had convinced some folks, whose disdain for registering was rooted in a disdain for both major political parties, to register. Kiran admitted that offering cookies while reminding them about global warming had worked for her. A couple of other class members admitted that flirting had helped them overcome some other resisters. After we laughed hard at the thought of me, the professor, flirting with potential registrants, the mood turned somber. Chris looked around the room and asked quietly, "How do we convince some of these people that this is important?" After they had all looked at each other, they looked toward me. Bright, sincere, authentic care for their fellow human beings and their country was imprinted upon their young faces.

I took a deep breath. "If the financial aid connection doesn't persuade them, if fear of losing the FDA doesn't persuade them, if flirting and cookies don't persuade them, then hand them one of these." At that I passed out the copies of the quote from the report I had typed earlier in the day. I closely watched those earnest faces in front of me twitch and crumple, their eyes tearing, their breath catching. I read it aloud.

"Five calls [from passengers on Flight 93] described the intent of passengers and surviving crew members to revolt against the hijackers. According to one call, they voted on whether to rush the terrorists in an attempt to retake the plane. They decided and acted."

"Remind them that people in the sky of Pennsylvania voted and then they acted together on behalf of all of us. They voted and acted so that we would continue to have the privilege to vote and to act. They voted, because that's what we do."

Quietly, we agreed to use this blunt instrument of a few simple words from a government report with great care. We agreed that it should be handled with the deft tenderness and respect that the dead deserved. As our voter registration drive wound down, we encountered several more disdainful potential voters. I, fortunately, only encountered one. However, this one, like every other one my students touched with this blunt instrument, quickly reevaluated his position and registered to vote.

Mary Lynne Gasaway

How Voting For Nixon Changed My (Love) Life

I voted to reelect Richard M. Nixon in 1972.

The admission of this fact was a source of embarrassment thirty-five years later—not because of my vote, but because my enthusiasm for the former president gave away my real age.

Richard M. Nixon was reelected on November 7, 1972, by one of the largest majorities in U.S. history. I was one of the millions of voters who reelected him. I had turned eighteen in July of that year, and was thrilled to be a part of the democratic process. Every vote counted, I had been told again and again, and I felt personally responsible for the president's huge victory. That euphoria changed, however, as news of the Watergate break-in surfaced over the next months, leading to Nixon's resignation in August of 1974. As years passed, it become more and more difficult to find anyone who would admit they had actually voted for Nixon—even though he'd been reelected by 60.7 percent of the popular vote.

Fast forward to Spring 2007. I was finishing my last year as a "mature" college student, having spent the previous seven years juggling teenaged children, a failing marriage, and a dying parent, all while setting high academic standards for myself. As an English major, I was taking a required expository writing class—and was lucky enough to be in a class with a low enrollment, which gave me plenty of opportunities to get to know the other students. As the semester progressed, I had to admit I was more and more interested in Dennis, the student sitting next to me. He was witty, charming, and smart, and I wanted to get to know him better. Finally, my life seemed to be settling down and I was ready to move forward. I'd met someone who I found very interesting.

In the following weeks, our class had lively discussions about a variety of topics, and one afternoon we were working in small groups in preparation for a class writing assignment. Our group of four was a little off-task, and we worked our way through a variety of topics, finally settling on former President Jimmy Carter as a topic of conversation. Dennis, who spoke like a true Democrat, impressed me with his thoughtful comments as the discussion continued, and a lively political exchange ensued. I was feeling very comfortable until, out of the blue, Dennis finished a sentence with the statement, ". . . of course, you wouldn't know—you're too young to remember that."

I looked at him closely. Was he serious? Was he fishing for my age? Was he laughing at me? I felt certain that he was a few years younger than I, yet I was not about to reveal my age. I was, after all, over 50, and if I was correct about Dennis being younger, that particular number might be a deal-breaker. My mind was racing to construct the perfect witty-yet-evasive answer.

"How old are *you*, Dennis?"

"I'm 48."

I hesitated. I was 52 years old, and there was no way I was going to admit it to this man. What should I say? I took a deep breath.

"I'm a little older than you," I said carefully. "But not a lot," I qualified quickly, flashing what I hoped was my most charming smile. I thought I'd come up with an answer that was honest but vague—the perfect combination.

The conversation continued and I relaxed, convinced that my secret was safe.

Weeks later, Dennis and I were dating. He was so much fun to be with, and I was having the time of my life. Lingering in the background, however, was my fear that he would find out how old I really was. I was flattering myself, believing that I looked younger than my age, and I didn't want the truth revealed. When our conversations periodically turned to subjects that might give away my age, I carefully steered them in another direction. The subject of my age never came up directly, and I was careful to avoid any subject that might bring it up.

One day, Dennis and I were discussing "firsts" in our lives, and I told the story of the first time I had voted in a presidential election. I proudly announced that I had been one of the first eighteen- to twenty-one-year olds to vote after the passage of the twenty-sixth amendment, and furthermore, I was one of the very few people he would ever meet who would openly admit to voting for Nixon. Even before the words were completely out of my mouth, I knew I was in trouble: as Dennis looked at me, I feared he was calculating what that meant, and I was right. He grinned, hesitated a moment while I stammered helplessly, and then he asked, "You do mean the reelection, right? Not his first election in 1968?" His impish grin said it all—he didn't care that there were a few years between us.

I had been right—this guy *was* special. And never before had I been as happy to admit that my first vote, in the 1972 presidential election, had been for Richard M. Nixon.

Candace Johnson

Reprinted by permission of Atlantic Feature Syndicate. ©1992 Atlantic Feature Syndicate.

WH SAID IT?

"I don't want to spend the rest of my life giving speeches."

—*Colin Powell*

"We must and we shall return to proven ways—not because they are old, but because they are true."

—*Barry Goldwater*

"At the end of your life, you will never regret not having passed one more test, not winning one more verdict or not closing one more deal. You will regret time not spent with a husband, a friend, a child, or a parent."

—*Barbara Bush*

"Speak softly and carry a big stick."

—*Theodore Roosevelt*

"Let not him who is houseless
pull down the house of another, but let him
work diligently and build one for himself,
thus by example assuring that his own shall
be safe from violence when built."

—*Abraham Lincoln*

"The business of
America is business"

—*Calvin Coolidge*

"All free governments
are managed by the combined
wisdom and folly of
the people."

—*James Garfield*

"The only legitimate
right to govern is an express
grant of power from
the governed."

—*Benjamin Harris*

My good friend and great Republican, Dick Nixon, and your charming wife, Pat; my running mate, that wonderful Republican who has served us so well for so long, Bill Miller and his wife, Stephanie; to Thurston Morton who's done such a commendable job in chairing this Convention; to Mr. Herbert Hoover, who I hope is watching; and to that—that great American and his wife, General and Mrs. Eisenhower; to my own wife, my family, and to all of my fellow Republicans here assembled, and Americans across this great Nation.

From this moment, united and determined, we will go forward together, dedicated to the ultimate and undeniable greatness of the whole man. Together—Together we will win.

I accept your nomination with a deep sense of humility. I accept, too, the responsibility that goes with it, and I seek your continued help and your continued guidance. My fellow Republicans, our cause is too great for any man to feel worthy of it. Our task would be too great for any man, did he not have with him the hearts and the hands of this great Republican Party, and I promise you tonight that every fiber of my being is consecrated to our cause; that nothing shall be lacking from the struggle that can be brought to it by enthusiasm, by devotion, and plain hard work.

In this world no person, no Party can guarantee anything, but what we can do and what we shall do is to deserve victory, and victory will be ours.

The good Lord raised this mighty Republic to be a home for the brave and to flourish as the land of the free—not to stagnate in the swampland of collectivism, not to cringe before the bullying of communism.

Now, my fellow Americans, the tide has been running against freedom. Our people have followed false prophets. We must, and we shall, return to proven ways—not because they are old, but because they are true. We must, and we shall, set the tides running again in the cause of freedom. And this party, with its every action, every word, every breath, and every heartbeat, has but a single resolve, and that is freedom—freedom made orderly for this Nation by our constitutional government; freedom under a government limited by the laws of nature and of nature's God; freedom balanced so that order lacking liberty [sic] will not become the slavery of the prison shell [cell]; balanced so that liberty lacking order will not become the license of the mob and of the jungle.

Now, we Americans understand freedom. We have earned it; we have lived for it, and we have died for it. This Nation and its people are freedom's model in a searching world. We can be freedom's missionaries in a doubting world. But, ladies and gentlemen, first we must renew freedom's mission in our own hearts and in our own homes.

During four futile years, the administration which we shall replace has—has distorted and lost that vision. It has talked and talked and talked and talked the words of freedom, but it has failed and failed and failed in the works of freedom.

Now, failures cement the wall of shame in Berlin. Failures blot the sands of shame at the Bay of Pigs. Failures mark the slow death of freedom in Laos. Failures infest the jungles of Vietnam. And failures haunt the houses of our once great alliances and undermine the greatest bulwark ever erected by free nations—the NATO community. Failures proclaim lost leadership, obscure purpose, weakening will, and the risk of inciting our sworn enemies to new aggressions and to new excesses.

And because of this administration we are tonight a world divided; we are a Nation becalmed. We have lost the brisk pace of diversity and the genius of individual creativity. We are plodding along at a pace set by centralized planning, red tape, rules without responsibility, and regimentation without recourse.

Rather than useful jobs in our country, our people have been offered bureaucratic "make work"; rather than moral leadership, they have been given bread and circuses. They have been given spectacles, and, yes, they've even been given scandals.

Tonight, there is violence in our streets, corruption in our highest offices, aimlessness amongst our youth, anxiety among our elders, and there's a virtual despair among the many who look beyond material success for the inner meaning of their lives. And where examples of morality should be set, the opposite is seen. Small men, seeking great wealth or power, have too often and too long turned even the highest levels of public service into mere personal opportunity.

Now, certainly, simple honesty is not too much to demand of men in government. We find it in most. Republicans demand it from everyone. They demand it from everyone no matter how exalted or protected his position might be. Now the—the growing menace in our country tonight, to personal safety, to life, to limb and property, in homes, in churches, on the playgrounds, and places of business, particularly in our great cities, is the mounting concern, or should be, of every thoughtful citizen in the United States.

Security from domestic violence, no less than from foreign aggression, is the most elementary and fundamental purpose of any government and a government that cannot fulfill this purpose is one that cannot long command the loyalty of its citizens.

History shows us—it demonstrates that nothing, nothing prepares the way for tyranny more than the failure of public officials to keep the streets safe from bullies and marauders.

Now, we Republicans see all this as more, much more, than the result of mere political differences or mere political mistakes. We see this as the result of a fundamentally and absolutely wrong view of man, his nature, and his destiny. Those who seek to live your lives for you, to take your liberties in return for relieving you of yours, those who elevate the state and downgrade the citizen must see ultimately a world in which earthly power can be substituted for Divine Will, and this Nation was founded upon the rejection of that notion and upon the acceptance of God as the author of freedom.

Now those who seek absolute power, even though they seek it to do what they regard as good, are simply demanding the right to enforce their own version of heaven on earth. They—and let me remind you, they are the very ones who always create the most hellish tyrannies. Absolute power does corrupt, and those who seek it must be suspect and must be opposed. Their mistaken course stems from false notions, ladies and gentlemen, of equality. Equality, rightly understood, as our founding fathers understood it, leads to liberty and to the emancipation of creative differences. Wrongly understood, as it has been so tragically in our time, it leads first to conformity and then to despotism.

Fellow Republicans, it is the cause of Republicanism to resist concentrations of power, private or public, which—which enforce such conformity and inflict such despotism. It is the cause of Republicanism to ensure that power remains in the hands of the people. And, so help us God that is exactly what a Republican President will do with the help of a Republican Congress.

It is further the cause of Republicanism to restore a clear understanding of the tyranny of man over man in the world at large. It is our cause to dispel the foggy thinking which avoids hard decisions in the delusion that a world of conflict will somehow mysteriously resolve itself into a world of harmony, if we just don't rock the boat or irritate the forces of aggression—and this is hogwash.

It is further the cause of Republicanism to remind ourselves, and the world, that only the strong can remain free, that only the strong can keep the peace.

Now, I needn't remind you, or my fellow Americans regardless of party, that Republicans have shouldered this hard responsibility and marched in this cause before. It was Republican leadership under Dwight Eisenhower that kept the peace, and passed along to this administration the mightiest arsenal for defense the world has ever known. And I needn't remind you that it was the strength and the [un]believable will of the Eisenhower years that kept the peace by using our strength, by using it in the Formosa Straits and in Lebanon and by showing it courageously at all times.

It was during those Republican years that the thrust of Communist imperialism was blunted. It was during those years of Republican leadership that this world moved closer, not to war, but closer to peace, than at any other time in the last three decades.

And I needn't remind you—but I will—that it's been during Democratic years that our strength to deter war has stood still, and even gone into a planned decline. It has been during Democratic years that we have weakly stumbled into conflict, timidly refusing to draw our own lines against aggression, deceitfully refusing to tell even our people of our full participation, and tragically, letting our finest men die on battlefields, unmarked by purpose, unmarked by pride or the prospect of victory.

Yesterday, it was Korea. Tonight, it is Vietnam. Make no bones of this. Don't try to sweep this under the rug. We are at war in Vietnam. And yet the President, who is the Commander-in-Chief of our forces, refuses to say—refuses to say, mind you, whether or not the objective over there is victory. And his Secretary of Defense continues to mislead and misinform the American people, and enough of it has gone by.

And I needn't remind you—but I will—it has been during Democratic years that a billion persons were cast into Communist captivity and their fate cynically sealed.

Today—Today in our beloved country we have an administration which seems eager to deal with communism in every coin known—from gold to wheat, from consulates to confidences, and even human freedom itself.

Now the Republican cause demands that we brand communism as the principal disturber of peace in the world today. Indeed, we should brand it as the only significant disturber of the peace, and we must make clear that until its goals of conquest are absolutely renounced and its relations with all nations tempered, communism and the governments it now controls are enemies of every man on earth who is or wants to be free.

Now, we here in America can keep the peace only if we remain vigilant and only if we remain strong. Only if we keep our eyes open and keep our guard up can we prevent war. And I want to make this abundantly clear: I don't intend to let peace or freedom be torn from our grasp because of lack of strength or lack of will—and that I promise you, Americans.

I believe that we must look beyond the defense of freedom today to its extension tomorrow. I believe that the communism which boasts it will bury us will, instead, give way to the forces of freedom. And I can see in the distant and yet recognizable future the outlines of a world worthy of our dedication, our every risk, our every effort, our every sacrifice along the way. Yes, a world that will redeem the suffering of those who will be liberated from tyranny. I can see—and I suggest that all thoughtful men must contemplate—the flowering of an Atlantic civilization, the whole of Europe reunified and freed, trading openly across its borders, communicating openly across the world.

Now, this is a goal far, far more meaningful than a moon shot.

It's a—It's a truly inspiring goal for all free men to set for themselves during the latter half of the twentieth century.

I can also see—and all free men must thrill to—the events of this Atlantic civilization joined by its great ocean highway to the United States. What a destiny! What a destiny can be ours to stand as a great central pillar linking Europe, the Americas, and the venerable and vital peoples and cultures of the Pacific. I can see a day when all the Americas, North and South, will be linked in a mighty system, a system in which the errors and misunderstandings of the past will be submerged one by one in a rising tide of prosperity and interdependence. We know that the misunderstandings of centuries are not to be wiped away in a day or wiped away in an hour. But we pledge, we pledge that human sympathy—what our neighbors to the South call an attitude of "simpatico"—no less than enlightened self-interest will be our guide.

And I can see this Atlantic civilization galvanizing and guiding emergent nations everywhere.

Now I know this freedom is not the fruit of every soil. I know that our own freedom was achieved through centuries, by unremitting efforts of brave and wise men. And I know that the road to freedom is a long and a challenging road. And I know also that some men may walk away from it, that some men resist challenge, accepting the false security of governmental paternalism.

And I—And I pledge that the America I envision in the years ahead will extend its hand in health, in teaching and in cultivation, so that all new nations will be at least encouraged—encouraged!—to go our way, so that they will not wander down the dark alleys of tyranny or the dead-end streets of collectivism.

My fellow Republicans, we do no man a service by hiding freedom's light under a bushel of mistaken humility.

I seek an America proud of its past, proud of its ways, proud of its dreams, and determined actively to proclaim them. But our example to the world must, like charity, begin at home.

In our vision of a good and decent future, free and peaceful, there must be room, room for deliberation of the energy and the talent of the individual; otherwise our vision is blind at the outset.

We must assure a society here which, while never abandoning the needy or forsaking the helpless, nurtures incentives and opportunities for the creative and the productive. We must know the whole good is the product of many single contributions.

And I cherish a day when our children once again will restore as heroes the sort of men and women, who, unafraid and undaunted, pursue the truth, strive to cure disease, subdue and make fruitful our natural environment and produce the inventive engines of production, science, and technology.

This Nation, whose creative people have enhanced this entire span of history, should again thrive upon the greatness of all those things which we, we as individual citizens, can and should do. And during Republican years, this again will be a nation of men and women, of families proud of their role, jealous of their responsibilities, unlimited in their aspirations—a Nation where all who can will be self-reliant.

We Republicans see in our constitutional form of government the great framework which assures the orderly but dynamic fulfillment of the whole man, and we see the whole man as the great reason for instituting orderly government in the first place.

We see—We see in private property and in economy based upon and fostering private property, the one way to make government a durable ally of the whole man, rather than his determined enemy. We see in the sanctity of private property the only durable foundation for constitutional government in a free society. And—And beyond that, we see, in cherished diversity of ways, diversity of thoughts, of motives and accomplishments. We don't seek to lead anyone's life for him. We only seek—only seek to secure his rights, guarantee him opportunity— guarantee him opportunity to strive, with government performing only those needed and constitutionally sanctioned tasks which cannot otherwise be performed.

We Republicans seek a government that attends to its inherent responsibilities of maintaining a stable monetary and fiscal climate, encouraging a free and a competitive economy and enforcing law and order. Thus, do we seek inventiveness, diversity, and creative difference within a stable order, for we Republicans define government's role where needed at many, many levels—preferably, though, the one closest to the people involved.

Our towns and our cities should come first then our counties, our states, our regional compacts and only then the national government. That, let me remind you, is the ladder of liberty, built by decentralized power. On it also we must have balance between the branches of government at every level.

Balance, diversity, creative difference: These are the elements of the Republican equation. Republicans agree—Republicans agree heartily to disagree on many, many of their applications, but we have never disagreed on the basic fundamental issues of why you and I are Republicans.

This is a Party. This Republican Party is a Party for free men, not for blind followers, and not for conformists.

In fact, in 1858 Abraham Lincoln said this of the Republican party—and I quote him, because he probably could have said it during the last week or so: "It was composed of strange, discordant, and even hostile elements"—end of the quote—in 1858. Yet—Yet all of these elements agreed on one paramount objective: To arrest the progress of slavery, and place it in the course of ultimate extinction.

Today, as then, but more urgently and more broadly than then, the task of preserving and enlarging freedom at home and of safeguarding it from the forces of tyranny abroad is great enough to challenge all our resources and to require all our strength.

Anyone who joins us in all sincerity, we welcome. Those who do not care for our cause, we don't expect to enter our ranks in any case. And—And let our Republicanism, so focused and so dedicated, not be made fuzzy and futile by unthinking and stupid labels.

I would remind you that extremism in the defense of liberty is no vice.

(Thank you. Thank you. Thank you. Thank you. Thank you.)

And let me remind you also that moderation in the pursuit of justice is no virtue.

Why the beauty of the very system we Republicans are pledged to restore and revitalize, the beauty of this Federal system of ours is in its reconciliation of diversity with unity. We must not see malice in honest differences of opinion, and no matter how great, so long as they are not inconsistent with the pledges we have given to each other in and through our Constitution.

Our Republican cause is not to level out the world or make its people conform in computer regimented sameness. Our Republican cause is to free our people and light the way for liberty throughout the world.

Ours is a very human cause for very humane goals.

This Party, its good people, and its unquenchable devotion to freedom, will not fulfill the purposes of this campaign, which we launch here and now, until our cause has won the day, inspired the world, and shown the way to a tomorrow worthy of all our yesteryears.

I repeat, I accept your nomination with humbleness, with pride, and you and I are going to fight for the goodness of our land.

Thank you.

A great moment in Republican history: American politician Theodore Roosevelt (center left), later the 26th President of the United States of America, with his men of the 1st Cavalry Volunteers, known as the "Rough Riders," on San Juan Hill during the Spanish-American War.

Trivia

1. Who was the only president to resign from office?

2. Who was the youngest president in American history?

3. Who was the only Republican to place third in a presidential election?

4. Who was the first presidential candidate to win over 60 percent of the popular vote?

5. Who was the oldest person to serve in the United States Senate?

6. Who was the last Republican presidential candidate to win the majority of the African American vote?

7. Who was the oldest man to be elected president?

8. Who was elected president with the most electoral votes?

9. What was the greatest number of convention ballots needed to nominate a Republican presidential candidate?

10. Who was the first woman to be elected to both the House and the Senate?

11. Who was the first African American to serve a full term in the United States Senate?

1. Richard M. Nixon in 1974

2. Theodore Roosevelt was forty-two when he became president following the assassination of William McKinley in 1901.

3. In 1912, William Howard Taft came behind both the Democratic candidate Woodrow Wilson and the Progressive candidate Theodore Roosevelt in both popular and electoral votes.

4. Warren G. Harding in 1920

5. James Strom Thurmond of South Carolina was 100 when he left office in 2003.

6. Herbert Hoover in 1932

7. Ronald Reagan was sixty-nine when he took the oath of office in 1981.

8. Ronald Reagan won 525 electoral votes in 1984. His opponent Walter Mondale won 13.

9. James A. Garfield was nominated on the 36th ballot in 1880.

10. Margaret Chase Smith of Maine, who served as a Representative 1940–1949 and as a Senator 1949–1973

11. Blanche Bruce of Mississippi, 1875–1881

Of Flags, Candles, and Friends

Ever since I confirmed one of her greatest nightmares—one of her sons growing up to be a Republican—my mom can often be seen shaking her head in sheer confusion or heard muttering something under her breath about my partisanship. As you can imagine, political conversations across the dinner table have made for some entertaining spectacles. Yes, she still tears up when she drives me to the airport so I can fly back to college; secretly, however, I know part of her is thinking, *Hallelujah! Now the only Republican left in the house is my husband, and he is a political pushover!* But in mid-September of 2007, I had a story to write my mom that I think made her proud of her "politically-challenged" son.

I was only thirteen and was some 3000 miles away from the tragic events of September 11, 2001. But I'll always remember my father running into my room to wake me up and rush me downstairs as if we were evacuating the house. The picture on the television screen made my legs weak, my feet numb. I'll never forget watching the North Tower fall. The image—the willow tree of smoke and debris—became ingrained in my memory forever. In disbelief, I remember asking my dad if the tower could actually collapse.

"It's happening right now, Zac. It's . . . it's . . . real. Please, go get ready for school." The look in his eyes was something I had never seen before. It was something I never wanted to see again.

Before the 2007–08 school year began, our University of Pennsylvania

College Republicans' executive board crafted an action plan for the months to follow. It included the typical fund-raisers and speaking engagements, the lunches with faculty members, and the debate-watching parties. The prospect of mobilizing Republicans on campus was exciting, but I knew that our organization could serve a greater purpose. As the leader of the organization, I was sure I could find a way to prove our mettle to the university community through something atypical, something completely new to Penn. If we could plan something that people on campus of any political affiliation could take part in, the Penn College Republicans could gain the respect we rightfully deserved. Shaping the schedule for the upcoming academic year, I did not realize that the most impactful contribution to Penn by the college Republicans would be made on September 11, 2007.

On September 10, over forty college Republicans headed to College Green at 10:00 PM to help build a 9-11 memorial. We got to work planting almost 3000 miniature American flags and chalking reminders throughout campus, such as "Always Remember 9-11." I have never seen a group of twenty-year-olds come together and work in such harmony, such unity. I think we Republicans knew the importance of our actions, what they meant not only to Penn, but also to those throughout the country affected by the atrocities of 9-11.

Philadelphia was engulfed in a misty haze for most of September 11, 2007. It was a haunting and sober mist, one that seemed to swallow the campus and remain longer than normal. As students and faculty came to College Green at around 9:00 PM, we handed out candles, lighting only several so that those present would have to pass their flame to another's candle. The 150 candles ran out quickly—over 200 people had come to witness the culmination to the day-long memorial. The pictures I have of the service, of fellow college Republicans, and even of those not a part of our organization, will always remind me of the inherent goodness of people.

At 9:11 PM, the service began with a cappella-version of the national anthem. A moment of silence followed. If any noise sounded from other parts of the campus or the city, I could not hear a thing. I saw nothing but radiating candles and the bowed faces of some of my best friends—people like me, whose children and grandchildren will one day ask them where they were when the towers fell. The sight caused me to shiver—a feeling that is difficult to explain, but one which we all know and share—the sensation that runs upward through the spine and causes tears to well. Josh, a fellow college Republican and volunteer New York firefighter, concluded the memorial service with a speech recalling the heroism and courage of two men in his company who perished while trying to save those still trapped in the World Trade Center. He spoke about the dynamism of these heroes, of the family and friends they left behind when they sacrificed their lives for people they did not know. As I listened to Josh's speech, the burning candle in my hand made me feel whole. Tears flowed freely down my cheeks.

I have always been proud of being a Republican and leading students with the same partisanship in a quest for respect on campus. In less than one year, I have brought congressmen, governors, senators, and presidential candidates to Penn. But when the clock strikes midnight on my undergraduate career, I am confident that the 9-11 memorial will remain my crowning achievement, the defining moment that won the Penn College Republicans the admiration we deserved. I have never felt so fulfilled, so respected as a Republican as on September 11, 2007. To see fellow college Republicans construct and then attend the memorial with other peers of many political leanings reconfirmed why this organization holds a dear place in my heart.

Even before the first line of the "Star Spangled Banner" was sung that night, I knew our memorial was something to write home to my mom about. Yes, we would still disagree on most issues, but I was sure she would also have a newfound respect for her Republican son and his organization because of what they did to remember the victims of 9-11. I know she was proud, and I think she cried, too.

Zac Byer

The
Big Switch

I was not always a Republican. As a matter of fact, like a lot of people I knew, I despised the Republican Party. I thought it was a party that did not care about black people. I was in college in Pennsylvania when a black Republican told me that he worked for Tom Ridge, who had just been reelected as governor of Pennsylvania. Well, I was not impressed by this young Republican and scolded him for being one. I told him that a black Republican was an oxymoron.

Despite my harsh criticism of him, he did something for me that no Democrat had ever done. He gave me an opportunity to grow in a way that eventually changed my life forever. It all began when he introduced me to Governor Ridge's chief of staff. He found me qualified for the job and hired me to work for the governor while I was still in law school. This unexpected opportunity provided to me by a Republican, even though I was Democrat, caused me to want to learn more about the Republican Party. What I learned from my research inspired me to switch from being a Democrat to being a Republican.

It was Republicans, not Democrats, who fought to free blacks from slavery and amended our Constitution to guarantee blacks freedom, citizenship, and the right to vote. It was Republicans who championed all civil rights legislation from the mid-1860s to the 1960s. It was Republicans who started the NAACP and the Historically Black Colleges and Universities (HBCUs).

I was astonished to learn that it was the Democrats who fought to keep blacks in slavery and started the Ku Klux Klan to lynch both black and white Republicans. It was the Democrats who passed the discriminatory Black Codes and Jim Crow laws, as well as fought against all civil rights legislation—following the Civil War through the modern civil rights era of the 1960s.

One thing that really surprised me is that it was a Republican, President Richard Nixon, who started enforcing affirmative action to make sure blacks were not discriminated against and could get jobs and contracts based on their qualifications—just the way I was given such a chance by a Republican. Unfortunately, it's the Democrats who have turned the original idea of affirmative action into an unfair quota system that even most blacks don't support. The knowledge I gained from my historical research and working with Republicans inspired me to become a leader in the National Black Republican Association, helping to return African Americans to their Republican Party roots.

Richard St. Paul

FOUR SCORE

WHSAID IT?

"Force is all-conquering,
but its victories
are short-lived."

—*Abraham Lincoln*

"Defeat doesn't finish
a man— quit does. A man is not
finished when he's defeated.
He's finished when he quits."

—*Richard Nixon*

"Next to the right of
liberty, the right of property
is the most important
individual right guaranteed
by The Constitution."

—*William Howard Taft*

"Prosperity is
only an instrument to
be used, not a deity
to be worshiped."

—*Calvin Coolidge*

"A government big enough
to give you everything you want is a
government big enough to take from
you everything you have."

—Gerald Ford

"Get mad,
then get over it."

—Colin Powell

"History does not long
entrust the care of freedom to
the weak or the timid."

—Dwight D. Eisenhower

"A vote is like a rifle;
its usefulness depends
on the character
of the user."

—Theodore Roosevelt

Richard M. Nixon
The Great Silent Majority
Delivered November 3, 1969

Good evening, my fellow Americans.

Tonight I want to talk to you on a subject of deep concern to all Americans and to many people in all parts of the world, the war in Vietnam.

I believe that one of the reasons for the deep division about Vietnam is that many Americans have lost confidence in what their Government has told them about our policy. The American people cannot and should not be asked to support a policy which involves the overriding issues of war and peace unless they know the truth about that policy.

Tonight, therefore, I would like to answer some of the questions that I know are on the minds of many of you listening to me.

How and why did America get involved in Vietnam in the first place?

How has this administration changed the policy of the previous Administration?

What has really happened in the negotiations in Paris and on the battlefront in Vietnam?

What choices do we have if we are to end the war?

What are the prospects for peace?

Now let me begin by describing the situation I found when I was inaugurated on January 20: The war had been going on for four years. Thirty-one thousand Americans had been killed in action. The training program for the South Vietnamese was beyond [behind] schedule. Five hundred and forty-thousand Americans were in Vietnam with no plans to reduce the number. No progress had been made at the negotiations in Paris and the United States had not put forth a comprehensive peace proposal.

The war was causing deep division at home and criticism from many of our friends, as well as our enemies, abroad.

In view of these circumstances, there were some who urged that I end the war at once by ordering the immediate withdrawal of all American forces. From a political standpoint, this would have been a popular and easy course to follow. After all, we became involved in the war while my predecessor was in office. I could blame the defeat, which would be the result of my action, on him—and come out as the peacemaker. Some put it to me quite bluntly: This was the only way to avoid allowing Johnson's war to become Nixon's war.

But I had a greater obligation than to think only of the years of my Administration, and of the next election. I had to think of the effect of my decision on the next generation, and on the future of peace and freedom in America, and in the world.

Let us all understand that the question before us is not whether some Americans are for peace and some Americans are against peace. The question at issue is not whether Johnson's war becomes Nixon's war. The great question is: How can we win America's peace?

Well, let us turn now to the fundamental issue: Why and how did the United States become involved in Vietnam in the first place? Fifteen years ago North Vietnam, with the logistical support of Communist China and the Soviet Union, launched a campaign to impose a Communist government on South Vietnam by instigating and supporting a revolution.

In response to the request of the Government of South Vietnam, President Eisenhower sent economic aid and military equipment to assist the people of South Vietnam in their efforts to prevent a Communist takeover. Seven years ago, President Kennedy sent 16,000 military personnel to Vietnam as combat advisers. Four years ago, President Johnson sent American combat forces to South Vietnam.

Now many believe that President Johnson's decision to send American combat forces to South Vietnam was wrong. And many others, I among them, have been strongly critical of the way the war has been conducted.

But the question facing us today is: Now that we are in the war, what is the best way to end it?

In January I could only conclude that the precipitate withdrawal of all American forces from Vietnam would be a disaster not only for South Vietnam but for the United States and for the cause of peace.

For the South Vietnamese, our precipitate withdrawal would inevitably allow the Communists to repeat the massacres which followed their takeover in the North 15 years before. They then murdered more than 50,000 people and hundreds of thousands more died in slave labor camps.

We saw a prelude of what would happen in South Vietnam when the Communists entered the city of Hue last year. During their brief rule there, there was a bloody reign of terror in which 3,000 civilians were clubbed, shot to death, and buried in mass graves.

With the sudden collapse of our support, these atrocities at Hue would become the nightmare of the entire nation and particularly for the million-and-a half Catholic refugees who fled to South Vietnam when the Communists took over in the North.

For the United States this first defeat in our nation's history would result in a collapse of confidence in American leadership not only in Asia but throughout the world.

Three American Presidents have recognized the great stakes involved in Vietnam and understood what had to be done.

In 1963 President Kennedy with his characteristic eloquence and clarity said,

"We want to see a stable Government there," carrying on the [a] struggle to maintain its national independence." We believe strongly in that. We are not going to withdraw from that effort. In my opinion, for us to withdraw from that effort would mean a collapse not only of South Vietnam but Southeast Asia. So we're going to stay there."[1]

President Eisenhower and President Johnson expressed the same conclusion during their terms of office.

For the future of peace, precipitate withdrawal would be a disaster of immense magnitude. A nation cannot remain great if it betrays its allies and lets down its friends. Our defeat and humiliation in South Vietnam without question would promote recklessness in the councils of those great powers who have not yet abandoned their goals of worlds conquest. This would spark violence wherever our commitments help maintain the peace—in the Middle East, in Berlin, eventually even in the Western Hemisphere. Ultimately, this would cost more lives. It would not bring peace. It would bring more war.

For these reasons I rejected the recommendation that I should end the war by immediately withdrawing all of our forces. I chose instead to change American policy on both the negotiating front and the battle front in order to end the war fought on many fronts. I initiated a pursuit for peace on many fronts. In a television speech on May 14, in a speech before the United Nations, on a number of other occasions, I set forth our peace proposals in great detail.

We have offered the complete withdrawal of all outside forces within one year. We have proposed a cease fire under international supervision. We have offered free elections under international supervision with the Communists participating in the organization and conduct of the elections as an organized political force. And the Saigon government has pledged to accept the result of the election.

We have not put forth our proposals on a take-it-or-leave-it basis. We have indicated that we're willing to discuss the proposals that have been put forth by the other side. We have declared that anything is negotiable, except the right of the people of South Vietnam to determine their own future.

At the Paris peace conference Ambassador Lodge has demonstrated our flexibility and good faith in 40 public meetings. Hanoi has refused even to discuss our proposals. They demand our unconditional acceptance of their terms which are that we withdraw all American forces immediately and unconditionally and that we overthrow the government of South Vietnam as we leave.

We have not limited our peace initiatives to public forums and public statements. I recognized in January that a long and bitter war like this usually cannot be settled in a public forum. That is why in addition to the public statements and negotiations, I have explored every possible private avenue that might lead to a settlement.

Tonight, I am taking the unprecedented step of disclosing to you some of our other initiatives for peace, initiatives we undertook privately and secretly because we thought we thereby might open a door which publicly would be closed.

I did not wait for my inauguration to begin my quest for peace. Soon after my election, through an individual who was directly in contact on a personal basis with the leaders of North Vietnam, I made two private offers for a rapid, comprehensive settlement. Hanoi's replies called in effect for our surrender before negotiations. Since the Soviet Union furnishes most of the military equipment for North Vietnam, Secretary of State Rogers, my assistant for national security affairs, Dr. Kissinger, Ambassador Lodge and I personally have met on a number of occasions with representatives of the Soviet Government to enlist their assistance in getting meaningful negotiations started. In addition, we have had extended discussions directed toward that same end with representatives of other governments which have diplomatic relations with North Vietnam.

None of these initiatives have to date produced results. In mid-July I became convinced that it was necessary to make a major move to break the deadlock in the Paris talks. I spoke directly in this office, where I'm now sitting, with an individual who had known Ho Chi Minh on a personal basis for 25 years. Through him I sent a letter to Ho Chi Minh. I did this outside of the usual diplomatic channels with the hope that with the necessity of making statements for propaganda removed, there might be constructive progress toward bringing the war to an end.

Let me read from that letter to you now:

"Dear Mr. President:

I realize that it is difficult to communicate meaningfully across the gulf of four years of war. But precisely because of this gulf I wanted to take this opportunity to reaffirm in all solemnity my desire to work for a just peace. I deeply believe that the war in Vietnam has gone on too long and delay in bringing it to an end can benefit no one, least of all the people of Vietnam. The time has come to move forward at the conference table toward an early resolution of this tragic war. You will find us forthcoming and open-minded in a common effort to bring the blessings of peace to the brave people of Vietnam. Let history record that at this critical juncture both sides turned their face toward peace rather than toward conflict and war."

I received Ho Chi Minh's reply on August 30, three days before his death. It simply reiterated the public position North Vietnam had taken at Paris and flatly rejected my initiative. The full text of both letters is being released to the press.

In addition to the public meetings that I have referred to, Ambassador Lodge has met with Vietnam's chief negotiator in Paris in 11 private sessions. And we have taken other significant initiatives which must remain secret to keep open some channels of communications which may still prove to be productive.

But the effect of all the public, private, and secret negotiations which have been undertaken since the bombing halt a year ago, and since this Administration came into office on January 20th, can be summed up in one sentence: No progress whatever has been made except agreement on the shape of the bargaining table.

Well, now, who's at fault? It's become clear that the obstacle in negotiating an end to the war is not the President of the United States. It is not the South Vietnamese Government. The obstacle is the other side's absolute refusal to show the least willingness to join us in seeking a just peace. And it will not do so while it is convinced that all it has to do is to wait for our next concession, and our next concession after that one, until it gets everything it wants.

There can now be no longer any question that progress in negotiation depends only on Hanoi's deciding to negotiate—to negotiate seriously. I realize that this report on our efforts on the diplomatic front is discouraging to the American people, but the American people are entitled to know the truth—the bad news as well as the good news—where the lives of our young men are involved.

Now let me turn, however, to a more encouraging report on another front. At the time we launched our search for peace, I recognized we might not succeed in bringing an end to the war through negotiations. I therefore put into effect another plan to bring peace—a plan which will bring the war to an end regardless of what happens on the negotiating front. It is in line with the major shift in U. S. foreign policy which I described in my press conference at Guam on July 25. Let me briefly explain what has been described as the Nixon Doctrine—a policy which not only will help end the war in Vietnam but which is an essential element of our program to prevent future Vietnams.

We Americans are a do-it-yourself people—we're an impatient people. Instead of teaching someone else to do a job, we like to do it ourselves. And this trait has been carried over into our foreign policy.

In Korea, and again in Vietnam, the United States furnished most of the money, most of the arms, and most of the men to help the people of those countries defend their freedom against Communist aggression.

Before any American troops were committed to Vietnam, a leader of another Asian country expressed this opinion to me when I was traveling in Asia as a private citizen. He said: "When you are trying to assist another nation defend its freedom, U.S. policy should be to help them fight the war, but not to fight the war for them."

Well in accordance with this wise counsel, I laid down in Guam three principles as guidelines for future American policy toward Asia. First, the United States will keep all of its treaty commitments. Second, we shall provide a shield if a nuclear power threatens the freedom of a nation allied with us or of a nation whose survival we consider vital to our security. Third, in cases involving other types of aggression we shall furnish military and economic assistance when requested in accordance with our treaty commitments. But we shall look to the nation directly threatened to assume the primary responsibility of providing the manpower for its defense.

After I announced this policy, I found that the leaders of the Philippines, Thailand, Vietnam, South Korea, other nations which might be threatened by Communist aggression, welcomed this new direction in American foreign policy.

The defense of freedom is everybody's business—not just America's business. And it is particularly the responsibility of the people whose freedom is threatened. In the previous Administration, we Americanized the war in Vietnam. In this Administration, we are Vietnamizing the search for peace.

The policy of the previous Administration not only resulted in our assuming the primary responsibility for fighting the war, but even more significant did not adequately stress the goal of strengthening the South Vietnamese so that they could defend themselves when we left.

The Vietnamization plan was launched following Secretary Laird's visit to Vietnam in March. Under the plan, I ordered first a substantial increase in the training and equipment of South Vietnamese forces. In July, on my visit to Vietnam, I changed General Abrams's orders, so that they were consistent with the objectives of our new policies. Under the new orders, the primary mission of our troops is to enable the South Vietnamese forces to assume the full responsibility for the security of South Vietnam. Our air operations have been reduced by over 20 per cent.

And now we have begun to see the results of this long-overdue change in American policy in Vietnam. After five years of Americans going into Vietnam we are finally bringing American men home. By December 15 over 60,000 men will have been withdrawn from South Vietnam, including 20 percent of all of our combat forces. The South Vietnamese have continued to gain in strength. As a result, they've been able to take over combat responsibilities from our American troops.

Two other significant developments have occurred since this Administration took office. Enemy infiltration, infiltration which is essential if they are to launch a major attack over the last three months, is less than 20 percent of what it was over the same period last year. And most important, United States casualties have declined during the last two months to the lowest point in three years.

Let me now turn to our program for the future. We have adopted a plan which we have worked out in cooperation with the South Vietnamese for the complete withdrawal of all U.S. combat ground forces and their replacement by South Vietnamese forces on an orderly scheduled timetable. This withdrawal will be made from strength and not from weakness. As South Vietnamese forces become stronger, the rate of American withdrawal can become greater.

I have not, and do not, intend to announce the timetable for our program, and there are obvious reasons for this decision which I'm sure you will understand. As I've indicated on several occasions, the rate of withdrawal will depend on developments on three fronts. One of these is the progress which can be, or might be, made in the Paris talks. An announcement of a fixed timetable for our withdrawal would completely remove any incentive for the enemy to negotiate an agreement. They would simply wait until our forces had withdrawn and then move in.

The other two factors on which we will base our withdrawal decisions are the level of enemy activity and the progress of the training programs of the South Vietnamese forces. And I am glad to be able to report tonight progress on both of these fronts has been greater than we anticipated when we started the program in June for withdrawal. As a result, our timetable for withdrawal is more optimistic now than when we made our first estimates in June.

Now this clearly demonstrates why it is not wise to be frozen in on a fixed timetable. We must retain the flexibility to base each withdrawal decision on the situation as it is at that time, rather than on estimates that are no longer valid. Along with this optimistic estimate,

I must in all candor leave one note of caution. If the level of enemy activity significantly increases, we might have to adjust our timetable accordingly.

However, I want the record to be completely clear on one point. At the time of the bombing halt just a year ago there was some confusion as to whether there was an understanding on the part of the enemy that if we stopped the bombing of North Vietnam, they would stop the shelling of cities in South Vietnam.

I want to be sure that there is no misunderstanding on the part of the enemy with regard to our withdrawal program. We have noted the reduced level of infiltration, the reduction of our casualties and are basing our withdrawal decisions partially on those factors. If the level of infiltration or our casualties increase while we are trying to scale down the fighting, it will be the result of a conscious decision by the enemy. Hanoi could make no greater mistake than to assume that an increase in violence will be to its advantage.

If I conclude that increased enemy action jeopardizes our remaining forces in Vietnam, I shall not hesitate to take strong and effective measures to deal with that situation. This is not a threat. This is a statement of policy which as Commander-in-Chief of our armed forces I am making and meeting my responsibility for the protection of American fighting men wherever they may be.

My fellow Americans, I am sure you can recognize from what I have said that we really only have two choices open to us if we want to end this war. I can order an immediate precipitate withdrawal of all Americans from Vietnam without regard to the effects of that action. Or we can persist in our search for a just peace through a negotiated settlement, if possible, or through continued implementation of our plan for Vietnamization, if necessary—a plan in which we will withdraw all of our forces from Vietnam on a schedule in accordance with our program as the South Vietnamese become strong enough to defend their own freedom.

I have chosen this second course. It is not the easy way. It is the right way. It is a plan which will end the war and serve the cause of peace, not just in Vietnam but in the Pacific and in the world.

In speaking of the consequences of a precipitous withdrawal, I mentioned that our allies would lose confidence in America. Far more dangerous, we would lose confidence in ourselves. Oh, the immediate reaction would be a sense of relief that our men were coming home. But as we saw the consequences of what we had done, inevitable remorse and divisive recrimination would scar our spirit as a people.

We have faced other crises in our history and we have become stronger by rejecting the easy way out and taking the right way in meeting our challenges. Our greatness as a nation has been our capacity to do what has to be done when we knew our course was right. I recognize that some of my fellow citizens disagree with the plan for peace I have chosen. Honest and patriotic Americans have reached different conclusions as to how peace should be achieved. In San Francisco a few weeks ago, I saw demonstrators carrying signs reading, "Lose in Vietnam, bring the boys home." Well, one of the strengths of our free society is that any American has a right to reach that conclusion and to advocate that point of view.

But as President of the United States, I would be untrue to my oath of office if I allowed the policy of this nation to be dictated by the minority who hold that point of view and who try to impose it on the nation by mounting demonstrations in the street. For almost 200 years, the policy of this nation has been made under our Constitution by those leaders in the Congress and the White House elected by all the people. If a vocal minority, however fervent its cause, prevails over reason and the will of the majority, this nation has no future as a free society.

And now, I would like to address a word, if I may, to the young people of this nation who are particularly concerned, and I understand why they are concerned, about this war.I respect your idealism. I share your concern for peace. I want peace as much as you do. There are powerful personal reasons I want to end this war. This week I will have to sign 83 letters to mothers, fathers, wives, and loved ones of men who have given their lives for America in Vietnam. It's very little satisfaction to me that this is only one-third as many letters as I signed the first week in office. There is nothing I want more than to see the day come when I do not have to write any of those letters.

I want to end the war to save the lives of those brave young men in Vietnam. But I want to end it in a way which will increase the chance that their younger brothers and their sons will not have to fight in some future Vietnam some place in the world.

And I want to end the war for another reason. I want to end it so that the energy and dedication of you, our young people, now too often directed into bitter hatred against those responsible for the war, can be turned to the great challenges of peace, a better life for all Americans, a better life for all people on this earth.

I have chosen a plan for peace. I believe it will succeed. If it does not succeed, what the critics say now won't matter. Or if it does succeed, what the critics say now won't matter. If it does not succeed, anything I say then won't matter.

I know it may not be fashionable to speak of patriotism or national destiny these days, but I feel it is appropriate to do so on this occasion. Two hundred years ago this nation was weak and poor. But even then, America was the hope of millions in the world. Today we have become the strongest and richest nation in the world, and the wheel of destiny has turned so that any hope the world has for the survival of peace and freedom will be determined by whether the American people have the moral stamina and the courage to meet the challenge of free-world leadership.

Let historians not record that, when America was the most powerful nation in the world, we passed on the other side of the road and allowed the last hopes for peace and freedom of millions of people to be suffocated by the forces of totalitarianism.

So tonight, to you, the great silent majority of my fellow Americans, I ask for your support. I pledged in my campaign for the Presidency to end the war in a way that we could win the peace. I have initiated a plan of action which will enable me to keep that pledge. The more support I can have from the American people, the sooner that pledge can be redeemed. For the more divided we are at home, the less likely the enemy is to negotiate at Paris.

Let us be united for peace. Let us also be united against defeat. Because let us understand—North Vietnam cannot defeat or humiliate the United States. Only Americans can do that.

Fifty years ago, in this room, and at this very desk, President Woodrow Wilson spoke words which caught the imagination of a war-weary world. He said: "This is the war to end wars." His dream for peace after World War I was shattered on the hard reality of great power politics. And Woodrow Wilson died a broken man.

Tonight, I do not tell you that the war in Vietnam is the war to end wars, but I do say this: I have initiated a plan which will end this war in a way that will bring us closer to that great goal to which—to which Woodrow Wilson and every American President in our history has been dedicated—the goal of a just and lasting peace.

As President I hold the responsibility for choosing the best path for that goal and then leading the nation along it.

I pledge to you tonight that I shall meet this responsibility with all of the strength and wisdom I can command, in accordance with your hopes, mindful of your concerns, sustained by your prayers.

Thank you and good night.

A great moment in Republican history: Dwight D. Eisenhower takes the Oath of Office as the President of the United States during his Inauguration, January 20, 1953, in Washington D.C. Also pictured is former president Harry S. Truman, left, and Richard M. Nixon, right.

Trivia

1. Who was the only American president associated with a soft drink?

2. Who was the only senator elected as a result of a write-in campaign?

3. Who was the first president to make a radio broadcast from the White House?

4. Which Presidents graduated from West Point?

5. Who was the only president to turn down offers to play professional football?

6. Who was the only Republican to run as the presidential nominee of the Democratic Party?

7. Who was the only grandson of a president to serve as president?

8. Who was the only Republican son of a president to serve as president?

9. When was the only time two Republican presidents ran against each other for the presidency?

10. Who was the first president to cross the country while in office?

11. Who was the first candidate who had been divorced to win the presidency?

1. Calvin Coolidge was well known for his love of Moxie, a soft drink popular in New England. Coolidge drank Moxie after being sworn in as president in his family home at Plymouth, Vermont.

2. James Strom Thurmond of South Carolina in 1954

3. Calvin Coolidge on February 22, 1924

4. Ulysses S. Grant in 1843 and Dwight D. Eisenhower in 1915

5. Gerald Ford declined to go pro upon graduating from the University of Michigan in 1935 so he could concentrate on a law career.

6. Horace Greeley in 1872

7. Benjamin Harrison, President 1889–1893, grandson of President William Henry Harrison.

8. George W. Bush, son of George H. W. Bush

9. In 1912, when Theodore Roosevelt ran as the Progressive candidate against William Howard Taft

10. Rutherford B. Hayes in 1880

11. Ronald Reagan in 1980

The American Soldier . . . a Heritage of Heroes

As Memorial Day and Veterans Day approach each year, I watch in anticipation of the changing seasons and celebrations. I am reminded of how thankful I am for the abundance we have in this great nation. Most Americans know, appreciate, and realize the sacrifices our nation's veterans have endured for our blessings of liberty.

Veterans throughout the history of our nation have answered the call to protect our freedoms because they believed in something other than themselves. They believed that freedom and liberty are worth fighting for and dying for if need be. And that beacon of light and hope shines today.

Times have certainly changed. Modern technology has eased the way in which our nation conducts business and the way our lives have been enriched by the blessings of a free and prosperous nation. In generations past, those men who fought to "form a more perfect union" believed in the ideals of a free people and a prosperous nation. Those Americans who fought in the trenches of France believed with a fervent heart that freedom belongs to each man and tongue. Those in the Ardennes and on Guadalcanal knew that nothing is more important than preserving liberty and defeating oppression. And those who fought in Korea, Vietnam, and Desert Storm realized the threats that existed yesterday will be prevalent tomorrow as well. And all understood, as do our veterans returning from Iraq and

Afghanistan, that nothing is more precious than preserving freedom today and ensuring the hope of liberty for tomorrow.

Our nation's veterans have come from all walks of life and backgrounds. When they answered the call to service, some were immigrants or farmers, and many were ordinary boys who, by the events set before them, were turned into extraordinary men. They came from New York to Chicago and Boston to San Diego. Our nation is the better because of them.

Today it is increasingly rare to find volunteers who are willing to temporarily give up comforts or careers for a diet of "beans and bullets." I am reminded of greatness by political leaders and all those who put aside those comforts to serve. And by doing so, they became heroes.

Back then they weren't called politicians; they were called servants—and for good reason. Presidents Eisenhower, Nixon, and George H. W. Bush, Senators Bob Dole and John McCain, and California's favorite son, Ronald Reagan, showed the light of liberty and the laurels of service.

Many have asked me lately, "How can I honor those who have served?" On Memorial Day and Veterans Day, you can honor a veteran you know by simply taking a minute to make a phone call and just say, "Thank you for your service." You can volunteer to place a few flags on veterans' graves. You can take a few moments to visit a veteran in one of our many VA hospitals across the nation. And in so doing, you'll bring tears to their eyes and joy to their hearts.

And the most important thing we can do before we shop for the latest item in the mall is to place that grand old flag on our front porches as we say a prayer for our veterans. The Stars and Strips convey the dreams, ideals, and hopes of those who have died and those still preserving freedom and the blessings of liberty.

So, on these days of remembrance and thanksgiving, I am thankful for those sacrifices made in Normandy, by my grandfather whom I never met. I am reminded of freedom by a German-Jewish immigrant named "Dorothy," who has serial numbers tattooed on her arm and a beautiful smile I shall never forget.

I am in awe of the power of freedom in every heart and tongue to instill hope, not just for Americans, but for the world. And may we all point to Liberty's light as she shines upon the path of those who yearn for freedom and for those who reach for her.

Shawn Black

R.E.S.P.E.C.T.

After my seventeen-year marriage ended in divorce, my goal was to concentrate on my career in financial management and to make certain my son got into a good college. I had no interest in dating, and I vowed "I'll never marry again."

Four months passed, and I was settling in. Life was good being a single mom and raising my sixteen-year-old son. However, lo and behold, my life took an unexpected turn.

One afternoon, I had an appointment with a customer who was interested in obtaining an equity loan. My heart leapt when he walked into my office and introduced himself. "I'm Nolan," he said. I couldn't help but stare as he readily poured himself a cup of coffee from a silver carafe I kept on a lateral file cabinet near my desk. His thick, fiery red hair fascinated me, as well as his impish grin and the bronze freckles scattered across his nose.

I tried my best to be professional as we discussed the real-estate properties he owned, why he needed the money, and what was required to apply for the loan. But I found myself blushing many times during our meeting. I wondered why I was acting like such an adolescent. At the end of the meeting, I shook Nolan's hand and thanked him for his business. I struggled to keep my composure, but it was too late. I heard myself giggling and accepting his invitation to meet him for coffee on Saturday morning.

Over coffee we shared remnants of our lives. He, too, was divorced and shared custody of a son. It didn't take long before we realized we enjoyed one another's company and had a lot in common—except for two things: he was a Republican, and I was a Democrat. Could these differences really matter? As we finished our coffee, I knew I was smitten, and so was he.

A year later, we were married. Marital bliss began with a blended family that consisted of our two sons, our two political parties, moving into a new house, and having a new designated polling place.

The year 1980 was our first Presidential election as a married couple. It was comical to see our mailbox stuffed with Ronald Reagan's Republican campaign literature and Jimmy Carter's Democratic campaign literature. The piles of mail we received from our political parties became a contest. Who'd receive the most mail each day? On most days, I won. "Wow, you Democrats sure like spending money," Nolan teased good-naturedly.

During our thirty years of marriage, we voted in more local, primary, and general elections in the state of California than I can recall. Our polling place was always at our neighborhood firehouse. After we cast our ballots, we'd walk home hand in hand, taking it in stride, knowing we'd more than likely canceled out each other's votes.

In 2000, I must admit I had high hopes for my party. I hung in there, eagerly waiting for the hanging chads to prevail. After the loss, Nolan gave me a hug and made a toast: "There's always 2004."

In 2003, we relocated to the state of Nevada due to Nolan's job being eliminated in California. We made certain we registered to vote in our new state of residence. We made no changes in our party affiliations. Sadly, my Democratic party lost in 2004. Again, we made a toast: "There's always 2008."

On Saturday, January 19, 2008, Nolan and I were elated to be participating in our first presidential caucuses. The news media announced that sites for the Nevada Republican and Democratic caucuses would be high schools, community centers, casinos, and cowboy bars. Gone were the days of casting our ballots at a neighborhood firehouse. We opted for the cowboy bar, but were told it wasn't in our precinct.

Our mailbox began to overflow with Democratic and Republican flyers and leaflets informing us that Nolan's Republican caucus would be held at 9:00 AM in a nearby high school, and my Democratic caucus would be held at 11:00 AM in the neighborhood community center.

After we attended our individual caucuses, we compared notes. As usual, lively, fun-filled banter ensued. He felt his Republican caucus was too chaotic. I thought my Democratic caucus was well organized. We agreed a primary election is better than a caucus and disagreed on who should be in the White House in 2008.

"I'm starving," Nolan said as we finished our feisty repartee.

"I'm not hungry at all," I said. "I had a large banana muffin and coffee at the caucus."

"Are you kidding me?" Nolan asked. "We didn't have anything to drink or eat at my caucus."

I smiled, and then replied, "I rest my case. Democrats rule!"

The only way to explain how we've had a harmonious two-party marriage for thirty years . . . Aretha Franklin says it best: "R.E.S.P.E.C.T."

Georgia A. Hubley

The Elephant and I Remember

It's been only a few days since the 2006 midterm elections. The Democrats have successfully taken over our country's house and senate seats, and I sorrowfully sit at my computer, licking my wounds.

Our founding faith finds American values constantly under assault, and this disturbs me greatly. Like most grandmothers, my thoughts tend to weigh heavily on morals and family issues. Abortion stops a beating heart, and children should have two parents working hard at their marriage. Drugs are a crime, kids shouldn't kill kids, and drunk drivers leave me fuming. I also find it fascinating that the "Terminator" flouts many core GOP values. And just for starters, imagine a hot potato issue that befuddles a few duly elected weak sisters who can't decide who or what they stand for. Oh, I have a million thoughts and memories in my duffle, but one in particular comes to mind.

My husband, Ken, and I were among the first to jump on the bandwagon of a brilliant and energetic young man as he announced his run for the Republican governor of our state. As his eastern district cochairpeople, we had helped to successfully bring him through his nomination, complete with a young elephant. No longer babes in the woods, we blossomed into seasoned campaigners, beginning each day with, "First we pray, then we work."

And the work was sometimes grueling. As a chairperson of Women on the Warpath (WOW), I rarely saw our children. Cell phones were not the rage then, so we installed phones in our cars to keep abreast of the home front and each other. Occasionally the campaign trail became dirty business as we quickly trounced on the mudslingers and their grist for the gossip mill. But we played the game astutely and wisely, keeping our powder dry, learning much, and having a ball.

As delegates to the National Republican Convention in San Francisco, we pinned our hopes on the presidential hopeful Barry Goldwater. It was the experience of a lifetime, allowing all of our Grand Old Party enthusiasm to unabashedly hang out with thousands of fellow Republicans. Yes, a few rowdy tipsters were in the Cow Palace, but much of the assemblage packed the workshops, offering smart and stimulating ideas. Nothing pleased me more than when our WOW league was snapped up by other states during roundtables and hospitality events.

Back home after the convention, the weekends were filled with activities for our candidate: celebrations, anniversaries, dedications, and holidays with parades, picnics, and high school marching bands. I followed the troops like a war-weary widow and acquainted myself with the newest WOW gals. The media seemed taken with the ladies all decked out in moccasins, feathered headbands, and simple rope-waisted beige shifts, an exuberant show of women participating in politics en masse. We brought the townsfolk out for a good look-see in every city and hamlet, and on television and front pages everywhere.

With the general election only two months off, Ken organized an enormous rally in the populous Tri-City area, where he was born and raised. An authentic stern-wheeler boat picked up our congressional delegation and gubernatorial candidate upstream on the Columbia River. They stopped at each community for handshakes and spiels while the local WOW gals passed around handouts, badges, and bumper stickers. The final stops included the largest city, with full frippery and fanfare designed for our, according to the polls, good-looking and popular front runner.

As the band played and hundreds of folks waited on the dock, a sudden squall caused the river boat to surge sideways and wrap around a bridge abutment. I had stayed behind with our children that day, feeling I needed to oversee the evening banquet and entertainment. Our son tore into the kitchen, screaming, "Dad's boat is sinking, Mom! It's sinking in the river!" Panic-stricken, we watched the news flash and sat glued to the television while they filmed the harrowing, but safe, rescue of all aboard.

You'd think it was intentional the way our opponent's cohorts billed it as a shrewd and shameless way to monopolize airtime and the front pages. Whatever . . . but none of us could help thinking the good Lord had a hand in intercepting near disaster that day. For you see, despite all the hoopla and headlines, our candidate was not only a handsome and savvy rising political star, he was also an ordained Lutheran minister.

Kathe Campbell

What It Means to Be Part of the GOP

WHSAID IT?

"You can tell a lot about a fellow's character by his way of eating jelly beans."

—*Ronald Reagan*

"America wasn't founded so that we could all be better. America was founded so we could all be anything we damned well pleased."

—*P.J. O'Rourke*

"Perseverance is the hard work you do after you get tired of doing the hard work you already did."

—*Newt Gingrich*

"We cannot forever hide the truth about ourselves, from ourselves."

—*John McCain*

Republican's Soul

"You can fool all of the people some of the time, and some of the people all of the time, but you cannot fool all of the people all of the time."

—*Abraham Lincoln*

"Read my lips: No new taxes."

—*George H. W. Bush*

"About the time we think we can make ends meet, somebody moves the ends."

—*Herbert Hoover*

"Patriotism means to stand by the country. It does not mean to stand by the president."

—*Theodore Roosevelt*

President Ronald Reagan
First Inaugural Address

"Putting America Back to Work"
Delivered January 20, 1981

Thank you. Thank you.

Senator Hatfield, Mr. Chief Justice, Mr. President, Vice President Bush, Vice President Mondale, Senator Baker, Speaker O'Neill, Reverend Moomaw, and my fellow citizens:

To a few of us here today this is a solemn and most momentous occasion. And, yet, in the history of our nation it is a commonplace occurrence. The orderly transfer of authority as called for in the Constitution routinely takes place as it has for almost two centuries and few of us stop to think how unique we really are. In the eyes of many in the world, this every-four-year ceremony we accept as normal is nothing less than a miracle.

Mr. President, I want our fellow citizens to know how much you did to carry on this tradition. By your gracious cooperation in the transition process you have shown a watching world that we are a united people pledged to maintaining a political system which guarantees individual liberty to a greater degree than any other. And I thank you and your people for all your help in maintaining the continuity which is the bulwark of our republic.

The business of our nation goes forward.

These United States are confronted with an economic affliction of great proportions. We suffer from the longest and one of the worst sustained inflations in our national history. It distorts our economic decisions, penalizes thrift, and crushes the struggling young and the fixed-income elderly alike. It threatens to shatter the lives of millions of our people. Idle industries have cast workers into unemployment, human misery, and personal indignity.

Those who do work are denied a fair return for their labor by a tax system which penalizes successful achievement and keeps us from maintaining full productivity. But great as our tax burden is, it has not kept pace with public spending. For decades we have piled deficit upon deficit, mortgaging our future and our children's future for the temporary convenience of the present. To continue this long trend is to guarantee tremendous social, cultural, political, and economic upheavals.

You and I, as individuals, can, by borrowing, live beyond our means, but for only a limited period of time. Why then should we think that collectively, as a nation, we are not bound by that same limitation?

We must act today in order to preserve tomorrow. And let there be no misunderstanding—we're going to begin to act beginning today. The economic ills we suffer have come upon us over several decades. They will not go away in days, weeks, or months, but they will go away. They will go away because we as Americans have the capacity now, as we have had in the past, to do whatever needs to be done to preserve this last and greatest bastion of freedom.

In this present crisis, government is not the solution to our problem;

government is the problem. From time to time we've been tempted to believe that society has become too complex to be managed by self-rule, that government by an elite group is superior to government for, by, and of the people. But if no one among us is capable of governing himself, then who among us has the capacity to govern someone else?

All of us together—in and out of government—must bear the burden. The solutions we seek must be equitable with no one group singled out to pay a higher price. We hear much of special interest groups. Well our concern must be for a special interest group that has been too long neglected. It knows no sectional boundaries, or ethnic and racial divisions, and it crosses political party lines. It is made up of men and women who raise our food, patrol our streets, man our mines and factories, teach our children, keep our homes, and heal us when we're sick—professionals, industrialists, shopkeepers, clerks, cabbies, and truck drivers. They are, in short, "We the People." This breed called Americans.

Well, this Administration's objective will be a healthy, vigorous, growing economy that provides equal opportunities for all Americans with no barriers born of bigotry or discrimination. Putting Americans back to work means putting all Americans back to work. Ending inflation means freeing all Americans from the terror of runaway living costs.

All must share in the productive work of this "new beginning," and all must share in the bounty of a revived economy.

With the idealism and fair play which are the core of our system and our strength, we can have a strong and prosperous America at peace with itself and the world. So as we begin, let us take inventory.

We are a nation that has a government—not the other way around. And this makes us special among the nations of the earth. Our Government has no power except that granted it by the people. It is time to check and reverse the growth of government which shows signs of having grown beyond the consent of the governed.

It is my intention to curb the size and influence of the Federal establishment and to demand recognition of the distinction between the powers granted to the Federal Government and those reserved to the states or to the people.

All of us—all of us need to be reminded that the Federal Government did not create the states; the states created the Federal Government.

Now, so there will be no misunderstanding, it's not my intention to do away with government. It is rather to make it work—work with us, not over us; to stand by our side, not ride on our back. Government can and must provide opportunity, not smother it; foster productivity, not stifle it. If we look to the answer as to why for so many years we achieved so much, prospered as no other people on earth, it was because here in this land we unleashed the energy and individual genius of man to a greater extent than has ever been done before.

Freedom and the dignity of the individual have been more available and assured in America than in any other place on earth. The price for this freedom at times has been high, but we have never been unwilling to pay that price.

It is no coincidence that our present troubles parallel and are proportionate to the intervention and intrusion in our lives that result from unnecessary and excessive growth of Government.

It is time for us to realize that we are too great a nation to limit ourselves to small dreams. We're not, as some would have us believe, doomed to an inevitable decline. I do not believe in a fate that will fall on us no matter what we do. I do believe in a fate that will fall on us if we do nothing.

So with all the creative energy at our command, let us begin an era of national renewal. Let us renew our determination, our courage, and our strength. And let us renew our faith and our hope. We have every right to dream heroic dreams.

Those who say that we're in a time when there are no heroes—they just don't know where to look. You can see heroes every day going in and out of factory gates. Others, a handful in number, produce enough food to feed all of us and then the world beyond. You meet heroes across a counter—and they're on both sides of that counter. There are entrepreneurs with faith in themselves and faith in an idea who create new jobs, new wealth and opportunity.

There are individuals and families whose taxes support the Government and whose voluntary gifts support church, charity, culture, art, and education. Their patriotism is quiet but deep. Their values sustain our national life.

Now I have used the words "they" and "their" in speaking of these heroes. I could say "you" and "your" because I'm addressing the heroes of whom I speak—you, the citizens of this blessed land. Your dreams, your hopes, your goals are going to be the dreams, the hopes, and the goals of this Administration, so help me God.

We shall reflect the compassion that is so much a part of your make-up. How can we love our country and not love our country-men—and loving them reach out a hand when they fall, heal them when they're sick, and provide opportunity to make them self-sufficient so they will be equal in fact and not just in theory? Can we solve the problems confronting us? Well the answer is an unequivocal and emphatic "Yes." To paraphrase Winston Churchill, I did not take the oath I've just taken with the intention of presiding over the dissolution of the world's strongest economy.

In the days ahead, I will propose removing the roadblocks that have slowed our economy and reduced productivity. Steps will be taken aimed at restoring the balance between the various levels of government. Progress may be slow—measured in inches and feet, not miles—but we will progress. It is time to reawaken this industrial giant, to get government back within its means, and to lighten our punitive tax burden. And these will be our first priorities, and on these principles there will be no compromise.

On the eve of our struggle for independence a man who might've been one of the greatest among the Founding Fathers, Dr. Joseph Warren, president of the Massachusetts Congress, said to his fellow Americans,

"Our country is in danger, but not to be despaired of. On you depends the fortunes of America. You are to decide the important question upon which rest the happiness and the liberty of millions yet unborn. Act worthy of yourselves."

Well I believe we, the Americans of today, are ready to act worthy of ourselves, ready to do what must be done to insure happiness and liberty for ourselves, our children, and our children's children. And as we renew ourselves here in our own land, we will be seen as having greater strength throughout the world. We will again be the exemplar of freedom and a beacon of hope for those who do not now have freedom.

To those neighbors and allies who share our freedom, we will strengthen our historic ties and assure them of our support and firm commitment. We will match loyalty with loyalty. We will strive for mutually beneficial relations. We will not use our friendship to impose on their sovereignty, for our own sovereignty is not for sale.

As for the enemies of freedom, those who are potential adversaries, they will be reminded that peace is the highest aspiration of the American people. We will negotiate for it, sacrifice for it; we will not surrender for it—now or ever. Our forbearance should never be misunderstood. Our reluctance for conflict should not be misjudged as a failure of will. When action is required to preserve our national security, we will act. We will maintain sufficient strength to prevail if need be, knowing that if we do so, we have the best chance of never having to use that strength.

Above all we must realize that no arsenal or no weapon in the arsenals of the world is so formidable as the will and moral courage of free men and women. It is a weapon our adversaries in today's world do not have. It is a weapon that we as Americans do have. Let that be understood by those who practice terrorism and prey upon their neighbors.

I am—I'm told that tens of thousands of prayer meetings are being held on this day; and for that I am deeply grateful. We are a nation under God, and I believe God intended for us to be free. It would be fitting and good, I think, if on each inaugural day in future years it should be declared a day of prayer.

This is the first time in our history that this ceremony has been held, as you've been told, on this West front of the Capitol.

Standing here, one faces a magnificent vista, opening up on this city's special beauty and history. At the end of this open mall are those shrines to the giants on whose shoulders we stand. Directly in front of me stands a monument to a monumental man. George Washington, father of our country. He was a man of humility who came to greatness reluctantly. He led America out of revolutionary victory into infant nationhood. Off to one side, the stately memorial to Thomas Jefferson. The Declaration of Independence flames with his eloquence. And then beyond the Reflecting Pool the dignified columns of the Lincoln Memorial. Whoever would understand in his heart the meaning of America will find it in the life of Abraham Lincoln.

Beyond those monuments—those monuments to heroism—is the Potomac River, and on the far shore the sloping hills of Arlington National Cemetery, with its row upon row of simple white markers bearing crosses or Stars of David. They add up to only a tiny fraction of the price that has been paid for our freedom.

Each one of those markers is a monument to the kind of hero I spoke of earlier. Their lives ended in places called Belleau Wood, the Argonne, Omaha Beach, Salerno, and halfway around the world on Guadalcanal, Tarawa, Pork Chop Hill, the Chosin Reservoir, and in a hundred rice paddies and jungles of a place called Vietnam.

Under one such marker lays a young man, Martin Treptow, who left his job in a small-town barber shop in 1917 to go to France with the famed Rainbow Division. There, on the Western front, he was killed trying to carry a message between battalions under heavy fire.

We're told that on his body was found a diary. On the flyleaf under the heading, "My Pledge," he had written these words:

"America must win this war. Therefore, I will work; I will save; I will sacrifice; I will endure; I will fight cheerfully and do my utmost, as if the issue of the whole struggle depended on me alone."

The crisis we are facing today does not require of us the kind of sacrifice that Martin Treptow and so many thousands of others were called upon to make. It does require, however, our best effort, and our willingness to believe in ourselves and to believe in our capacity to perform great deeds; to believe that together with God's help we can and will resolve the problems which now confront us.

And after all, why shouldn't we believe that? We are Americans.

God bless you and thank you. Thank you very much.

A great moment in Republican history: President Richard Nixon's historic February 1972 meeting with Chairman Mao Zedong, normalizing diplomatic relations between the United States and China.

Trivia

1. Who was the first president to win the Nobel Peace Prize?

2. Who was the first Jewish cabinet secretary?

3. Who was the only secretary of the treasury to serve three presidents?

4. What was the "smoke-filled room"?

5. Who was the "Great Communicator"?

6. When was the first permanent national party headquarters established in Washington, D.C.?

7. When did the Republican Party first capture both houses of Congress?

8. Who was the only Republican to serve as Speaker of the House and vice president?

9. Where does the term "boom" come from in American politics?

10. Who was the first modern campaign manager?

11. What is a "front porch campaign"?

1. Theodore Roosevelt in 1906, for brokering an end to the Russo-Japanese War

2. Oscar Solomon Straus, Secretary of Commerce and Labor under Theodore Roosevelt, 1906–1909

3. Andrew Mellon served as Secretary of the Treasury for Warren G. Harding, Calvin Coolidge, and Herbert Hoover, 1921–1932.

4. Room 404 of Chicago's Blackstone Hotel where a group of Republican leaders meeting during the 1920 convention decided that Senator Warren G. Harding of Ohio should be the party's nominee for the presidency

5. Ronald Reagan

6. The Republican National Committee was settled in Washington by RNC Chair Will Hayes in 1918.

7. 1860, with 31 of 50 Senators and 105 of 178 Representatives. This, with the concurrent election of Abraham Lincoln as president, led to southern secession and the outbreak of the Civil War.

8. Schuyler Colfax of Indiana, Speaker 1863–1869, Vice President 1969–1873

9. Joseph B. McCullaugh of the *St. Louis Globe-Democrat* referring to the 1880 third term movement for Ulysses S. Grant, called it a "boom," drawing the word from the name Mississippi riverboat pilots gave to an overflowing river

10. Marcus Alonzo Hanna of Ohio. Managing William McKinley's campaign in 1896, he spent more money than would be spent again until 1920. The Republican Party distributed 200 to 300 million copies of 275 items in twelve languages weighing 2,000 tons.

11. A presidential candidate stays at home and greets visitors on his "front porch." Famous "front porch" campaigns include those of James Garfield in 1880, William McKinley in 1896, and Warren G. Harding in 1920.

Watergate: The Warm Fuzzies

Sounding like a boy who had just discovered which classmate squealed about a locker break-in, my husband, Steve, asked, "Did you hear they announced the identity of Deep Throat?"

Since my husband is a Watergate-aficionado from way back, I was not surprised that he would learn before I did the news that the legendary Watergate source, "Deep Throat," was identified as W. Mark Felt.

For me, Watergate is a teary subject. Not because Nixon resigned humiliated and scandalized while I was navigating junior high school, attending my first sock hop, and wearing magnificently wide bell-bottom pants. No, Watergate draws a lump in my throat because it connects the important men in my life.

A few years ago, when my son, Jack, was eleven, he told me he had to make a school poster about Watergate. I grinned and thought, *He is his father's son. He is his grandfather's grandson. And the cosmic stars are in alignment.*

When my husband—a highly loveable techno-geek—was a teen in the early seventies, he recorded the televised Watergate reports on audiocassettes. Dangling a microphone in front of the speaker of his family's Zenith TV, he created his own "Watergate tapes" via whirling recorder. Steve still has the cartridges he had labeled "Impeachment—The Vote," "President's Resignation," and "Ford's Speech at Home." When our son said his poster topic was Watergate, I thought immediately of his father's antiquated tapes. After all these years, they would come in handy.

I also remembered Steve's diary from the early seventies—not a memoir of an angst-ridden thirteen-year-old, but a diary of a current-events-driven youth. He didn't chronicle unrequited love, but instead, facts about Watergate. His journal from his early teen years contains notes about the break-in, jottings about an erased tape, and an entry titled "Nixon resigned today."

As Jack searched the Web for photos of Nixon to decorate his poster, I fell into heavy Watergate-remembrance mode. Before me flashed my late father (the "Jack" for whom my son is named)—the grandfather my son has never known because he'd died four years before his birth.

Every night of those Watergate years, after returning home from his job as an electrical engineer at Purdue University, my dad sat in his avocado-green La-Z-Boy and watched the televised senate hearings. He was a current-events kind of guy, too. And although back then I knew the gist of Watergate, I preferred to watch *The Waltons* in another room.

From 1972 through 1974, Watergate was in my family's living room (every American family's living room) on the nightly news with John Chancellor, on the radio between Elton John and Bachman-Turner Overdrive, pounded daily in newspapers, and analyzed in my father's copies of *U.S. News & World Report*. But I read *Seventeen* and drooled over Robert Redford in *The Sting* and *The Way We Were*. I was into fluff. Watergate was a "dad thing."

Little did I know that a boy across town was recording every word of Watergate and that I would marry him one day, and years later, our son would listen to those tapes and learn not only about history, but also about his father's burgeoning love of politics.

I have to confess that the men in my life have saved me from complete ignorance of our government, whether I wanted them to or not. On the fringes of my years have been my father's and husband's intense interests in democracy (from different sides of the fence, though—my father was a Democrat, and Steve is a Republican). I bashfully admit, without them, I would be a political ostrich.

Of course, rounding out swings both ways. My love of the arty side of life has kept Steve from being consumed by the world's more weighty wheels. Without me, he'd need a twelve-step political-operative-addiction program.

I watched my son, heir to the techno-geek gene, digitally record an excerpt of Nixon's resignation speech from his father's old cassette to play with his Watergate poster.

"Your grandfather would have loved your project," I told him.

"I never knew him," my boy said pensively.

Did he, like I, feel the cosmic alignment of the universe?

In 1973, who knew it would take more than thirty years to learn who Deep Throat was . . . and that Watergate would one day warm the cockles of my heart?

Angie Klink

"I Like Ike"

In 1952, I lived in a sleepy town in southern Florida that had an exotic bird farm for tourists, a pineapple plantation amid acres of cattle ranches, and a two-story red brick schoolhouse at the end of Main Street. Not much was happening . . . until General Dwight D. Eisenhower announced he was running as the Republican candidate for president of the United States.

My eighth-grade teacher, Mrs. McCall, decided our social studies lessons prior to the November election should focus on researching the presidential candidates and holding a mock election in class when the nation voted. Since people didn't have television sets and computers back then, radios and newspapers supplied the news. When I saw a picture of General Eisenhower, I liked his uniform and his wide grin, and decided if he could lead troops as a general, he could lead the nation as our president. I joined the class group supporting Eisenhower while other classmates supported the Democratic opponent, Adlai Stevenson.

We busied ourselves in the school library and wrote biographies of General Eisenhower and Mr. Stevenson. We decorated our classroom bulletin boards with pictures and profiles of these accomplished men. Many of us wore campaign buttons advertising our candidates, including I LIKE IKE buttons. Campaign signs sprouted up in our classroom and around town. A few of us worked on the campaign speeches we would give before the students voted.

As the November election drew closer, I practiced my speech supporting Eisenhower. When the day for campaign speeches arrived, I was nervous about talking in front of my classmates. I feared Eugenia would sneer at me from the front row. I worried that Murphy would make me giggle with his silly antics. I expected Mrs. McCall would continue to frown with disapproval. When it was my turn, I walked to the podium, stood tall, and spoke with conviction about why I liked Ike. A lady carrying a big camera slipped into the classroom and squinted while she snapped several pictures of me giving my speech. I tried not to be distracted . . . but I was. Afterward, the lady took notes while she talked with my teacher.

My parents were surprised when they opened the local paper the next morning and saw the picture of me giving my speech. They told me they were proud. Even Mrs. McCall seemed pleased when she showed the picture to the class. The next day we held our mock election. General Eisenhower won by a landslide. Several students congratulated me for helping Ike win.

I thought that would be the end of the attention Ike brought me . . . but I was wrong.

Two months later the mailman delivered a letter addressed to me. I rarely got mail, unless my grandmother sent me a dollar in a birthday card. The return address was simply "The White House." Inside, under a black drawing of the White House, was a typed letter thanking me for campaigning for General Eisenhower . . . who was now President Eisenhower. It was personally signed by his wife, Mamie Eisenhower, our new First Lady, who was famous for the bangs on her forehead.

When I took my impressive letter to class, Mrs. McCall and the students were amazed that the wife of our new president wrote to me. The following day, the lady with the camera came to our class again. The next day my picture appeared in the newspaper. I was holding up my letter and standing next to Mrs. McCall, who was *smiling* at the camera. People wondered how Mrs. Eisenhower knew I had campaigned for her husband and where she got my name and address. It remains a mystery.

When I decided that "I Like Ike," I never dreamed my support of the Republican candidate would bring me fleeting fame in a sleepy, Florida town.

Miriam Hill

The Speech That Landed Barbara Bush in My Mailbox

Having just graduated from high school, I sat mesmerized by the television screen as First Lady Barbara Bush delivered the commencement address "Choices & Change" at Wellesley College on June 1, 1990. A great admirer of First Ladies even at age eighteen, I had followed the controversy and conflict that had dogged the lead-up to Mrs. Bush's appearance.

Some of the students at the historic all-female college had publicly expressed their opposition to Mrs. Bush's having been chosen as commencement speaker. They felt that she did not represent their modern perspective as independent-minded women because she had quit college to marry George Bush and had achieved notoriety only because of his fame.

I disagreed with these young women, and even more so as the First Lady proceeded through her speech. She spoke of the universal importance of the choices we make in life and how every moment is precious and worthy of being embraced.

I absorbed Mrs. Bush's words as if gulping cool water into my parched body. There wasn't a partisan message she sought to impart, but rather a comment on what it means to be a human being. Isn't that in essence what politics are supposed to be about anyway—living with ourselves and others in harmony and cohesion?

In particular, one of Mrs. Bush's passages illuminated my mind. She said, ". . . as important as your obligations as a doctor, lawyer, or business leader will be, you are a human being first and those human connections—with spouses, with children, with friends—are the most important investments you will ever make.

"At the end of your life, you will never regret not having passed one more test, not winning one more verdict, or not closing one more deal. You will regret time not spent with a husband, a child, a friend, or a parent."

The First Lady's timeless words instilled in me a rare sensitivity that I hadn't had before. She encouraged me to look around and evaluate my own human connections: with my parents, my high school friends, and others, most of whom I would soon be leaving when I went off to college, and from there, off into the adventure of my life where I would make even more connections. She taught me to see how we, indeed, are the glorious sum of those human connections.

Little did I know then that, in addition to helping me prioritize my ideals and life goals, Mrs. Bush's words would eventually lead me down one of my career paths.

Fast-forward two years. I was now a communications major at Marymount University, just across the river from The White House, where Mrs. Bush currently lived. During the spring semester, I was taking a "Writing for the Media" course, and one of our assignments was to craft a speech for someone we greatly admired. My mind immediately returned to Mrs. Bush and her rousing speech at Wellesley.

I decided to take a crack at writing my own commencement address for the First Lady. I did some research and learned that Mrs. Bush was scheduled to deliver the upcoming commencement address at Marquette University. I decided to tailor my speech for that event.

I reread the Wellesley speech for inspiration and then launched into my own text on Mrs. Bush's behalf. The focus of my speech was "change and courage for the young at heart." Thanks to Mrs. Bush's exhilarating example as an energetic mother and grandmother to a nation, the concept of remaining young at heart, regardless of numerical age, was important to me even at twenty years old.

Putting myself into Mrs. Bush's mindset as best as I could, I wrote of the courage we must have to face the changes and challenges of life. I spoke of the greatness that comes when we embrace these changes and challenges. I spoke of the greatness that comes when we embrace the human connections, which Mrs. Bush spoke so movingly about in her Wellesley speech, and I spoke of what it means to be young at heart.

Picturing Mrs. Bush delivering my speech, I wrote: "I wish I could tell you that you will never get hurt, never have heartache in your lives, but then I would not be telling you the truth. Even the Wizard told the Tin Man that 'hearts will never be practical until they can be made unbreakable.' But if you remember, he also said that 'a heart is not judged by how much you love, but how much you are loved by others.' Because of this, I hope that you will always put your families and friends first in your lives.

"Your 'human connections' are most important, and you should cherish them greatly, because when your time runs out on this earth, it will be too late to go back."

I then excerpted my favorite passage from the Wellesley speech, quoted above, feeling that the morsels of profound emotion and guidance it offered were important enough to bear repeating word for word.

I earned an A+ on the speech, and my professor suggested that I send it to Mrs. Bush at The White House. The thought of interacting with the First Lady even by mail thrilled me. So, before I went home for the summer, I wrote a letter to Mrs. Bush, telling her about our assignment, and mailed it off with a copy of my speech.

I didn't give the letter much more thought until a hot day in July when Barbara Bush's name landed in my mailbox on an envelope from The White House. Inside was a letter from the First Lady, which reads, in part:

"What a very good Marquette commencement speech you wrote with me in mind, and how impressed I am by your talent and enterprise! The central ideas you expressed so well were also important in my remarks, and I am gratified to know a gifted young person like you shares the values that mean so much to me.

"Thank you so much for thinking of me in such an eloquent way, and please keep writing. George Bush and I love to be reminded—as you have reminded me—that America's future is in very good hands."

Once again, Mrs. Bush's words—this time directed just to me—sent a wave of inspiration and encouragement throughout me. Her most influential words were "Please keep writing."

Three years later, with the then former First Lady's message still strong on my mind, I wrote my first book, *Corresponding with History: The Art and Benefits of Collecting Autographs.* In addition to the how-to of the hobby, the theme running throughout the book was its educational benefits. As a tribute to Mrs. Bush, her letter to me was the very first illustration in the book, allowing, I hoped, her words, and now mine, to further inspire other young people to chase their dreams and treasure their special human connections.

John E. Schlimm II

Reprinted by permission of Atlantic Feature Syndicate ©2006 Atlantic Feature Syndicate.

Republican's Soul

WHSAID IT?

"When you play, play hard; when you work, don't play at all."
—*Theodore Roosevelt*

"Don't expect to build up the weak by pulling down the strong."
—*Calvin Coolidge*

"A people that values its privileges above its principles soon loses both."
—*Dwight Eisenhower*

"When the President does it, that means it's not illegal."
—*Richard Nixon*

"To those of you who received honors, awards, and distinctions, I say, well done. And to the C students, I say, you, too, can be president of the United States."

—*George W. Bush*

"Whatever you are, be a good one."

—*Abraham Lincoln*

"The greatest honor history can bestow is that of peacemaker."

—*Richard Nixon*

"Government does not solve problems; it subsidizes them."

—*Ronald Reagan*

President George H. W. Bush

Address to the Nation on Invasion of Iraq

"While the World Waited...."

Delivered January 16, 1991

Just two hours ago, allied air forces began an attack on military targets in Iraq and Kuwait. These attacks continue as I speak. Ground forces are not engaged.

This conflict started August 2nd when the dictator of Iraq invaded a small and helpless neighbor. Kuwait—a member of the Arab League and a member of the United Nations—was crushed; its people, brutalized. Five months ago, Saddam Hussein started this cruel war against Kuwait. Tonight, the battle has been joined.

This military action, taken in accord with United Nations resolutions and with the consent of the United States Congress, follows months of constant and virtually endless diplomatic—diplomatic activity on the part of the United Nations, the United States, and many, many other countries. Arab leaders sought what became known as an Arab solution, only to conclude that Saddam Hussein was unwilling to leave Kuwait. Others traveled to Baghdad in a variety of efforts to restore peace and justice. Our Secretary of State, James Baker, held an historic meeting in Geneva, only to be totally rebuffed. This past weekend, in a last-ditch effort, the Secretary-General of the United Nations went to the Middle East with peace in his heart—his second such mission. And he came back from Baghdad with no progress at all in getting Saddam Hussein to withdraw from Kuwait.

Now the 28 countries with forces in the Gulf area have exhausted all reasonable efforts to reach a peaceful resolution—have no choice but to drive Saddam from Kuwait by force. We will not fail.

As I report to you, air attacks are underway against military targets in Iraq. We are determined to knock out Saddam Hussein's nuclear bomb potential. We will also destroy his chemical weapons facilities. Much of Saddam's artillery and tanks will be destroyed. Our operations are designed to best protect the lives of all the coalition forces by targeting Saddam's vast military arsenal. Initial reports from General Schwarzkopf are that our operations are proceeding according to plan.

Our objectives are clear: Saddam Hussein's forces will leave Kuwait. The legitimate government of Kuwait will be restored to its rightful place, and Kuwait will once again be free. Iraq will eventually comply with all relevant United Nations resolutions, and then, when peace is restored, it is our hope that Iraq will live as a peaceful and cooperative member of the family of nations, thus enhancing the security and stability of the Gulf.

Some may ask: Why act now? Why not wait? The answer is clear: The world could wait no longer. Sanctions, though having some effect, showed no signs of accomplishing their objective. Sanctions were tried for well over five months, and we and our allies concluded that sanctions alone would not force Saddam from Kuwait.

While the world waited, Saddam Hussein systematically raped, pillaged, and plundered a tiny nation, no threat to his own. He subjected the people of Kuwait to unspeakable atrocities—and among those maimed and murdered, innocent children.

While the world waited, Saddam sought to add to the chemical weapons arsenal he now possesses, an infinitely more dangerous weapon of mass destruction—a nuclear weapon.

And while the world waited, while the world talked peace and withdrawal, Saddam Hussein dug in and moved massive forces into Kuwait.

While the world waited, while Saddam stalled, more damage was being done to the fragile economies of the Third World, emerging democracies of Eastern Europe, to the entire world, including to our own economy.

The United States, together with the United Nations, exhausted every means at our disposal to bring this crisis to a peaceful end. However, Saddam clearly felt that by stalling and threatening and defying the United Nations, he could weaken the forces arrayed against him.

While the world waited, Saddam Hussein met every overture of peace with open contempt.

While the world prayed for peace, Saddam prepared for war.

I had hoped that when the United States Congress, in historic debate, took its resolute action, Saddam would realize he could not prevail and would move out of Kuwait in accord with the United Nation resolutions. He did not do that. Instead, he remained intransigent, certain that time was on his side.

Saddam was warned over and over again to comply with the will of the United Nations: Leave Kuwait, or be driven out. Saddam has arrogantly rejected all warnings. Instead, he tried to make this a dispute between Iraq and the United States of America.

Well, he failed. Tonight, 28 nations—countries from 5 continents, Europe and Asia, Africa, and the Arab League—have forces in the

Gulf area standing shoulder to shoulder against Saddam Hussein. These countries had hoped the use of force could be avoided. Regrettably, we now believe that only force will make him leave.

Prior to ordering our forces into battle, I instructed our military commanders to take every necessary step to prevail as quickly as possible, and with the greatest degree of protection possible for American and allied service men and women. I've told the American people before that this will not be another Vietnam, and I repeat this here tonight. Our troops will have the best possible support in the entire world, and they will not be asked to fight with one hand tied behind their back. I'm hopeful that this fighting will not go on for long and that casualties will be held to an absolute minimum.

This is an historic moment. We have in this past year made great progress in ending the long era of conflict and cold war. We have before us the opportunity to forge for ourselves and for future generations a new world order—a world where the rule of law, not the law of the jungle, governs the conduct of nations. When we are successful—and we will be—we have a real chance at this new world order, an order in which a credible United Nations can use its peacekeeping role to fulfill the promise and vision of the U.N.'s founders.

We have no argument with the people of Iraq. Indeed, for the innocents caught in this conflict, I pray for their safety. Our goal is not the conquest of Iraq. It is the liberation of Kuwait. It is my hope that somehow the Iraqi people can, even now, convince their dictator that he must lay down his arms, leave Kuwait, and let Iraq itself rejoin the family of peace-loving nations.

Thomas Paine wrote many years ago: "These are the times that try men's souls." Those well-known words are so very true today. But even as planes of the multinational forces attack Iraq, I prefer to think of peace, not war. I am convinced not only that we will prevail but that out of the horror of combat will come the recognition that no nation can stand against a world united, no nation will be permitted to brutally assault its neighbor.

No President can easily commit our sons and daughters to war. They are the Nation's finest. Ours is an all-volunteer force, magnificently trained, highly motivated. The troops know why they're there. And listen to what they say, for they've said it better than any President or Prime Minister ever could.

Listen to Hollywood Huddleston, Marine lance corporal. He says, "Let's free these people, so we can go home and be free again." And he's right. The terrible crimes and tortures committed by Saddam's henchmen against the innocent people of Kuwait are an affront to mankind and a challenge to the freedom of all.

Listen to one of our great officers out there, Marine Lieutenant General Walter Boomer. He said: "There are things worth fighting for. A world in which brutality and lawlessness are allowed to go unchecked isn't the kind of world we're going to want to live in."

Listen to Master Sergeant J.P. Kendall of the 82d Airborne: "We're here for more than just the price of a gallon of gas. What we're doing is going to chart the future of the world for the next 100 years. It's better to deal with this guy now than five years from now."

And finally, we should all sit up and listen to Jackie Jones, an Army lieutenant, when she says, "If we let him get away with this, who knows what's going to be next?"

I have called upon Hollywood and Walter and J.P. and Jackie and all their courageous comrades-in-arms to do what must be done. Tonight, America and the world are deeply grateful to them and to their families. And let me say to everyone listening or watching tonight: When the troops we've sent in finish their work, I am determined to bring them home as soon as possible.

Tonight, as our forces fight, they and their families are in our prayers. May God bless each and every one of them, and the coalition forces at our side in the Gulf, and may he continue to bless our nation, the United States of America.

A great moment in Republican history: President Ronald Reagan challenges Soviet leader Mikhail Gorbachev to "tear down this wall" at the Brandenburg Gate of the Berlin Wall on June 12, 1987.

Trivia

1. Who was the first Republican president?

2. Which Republican was originally the leader of a liberal union?

3. How many Republican presidents died in office?

4. Which party, the Republicans or Democrats, had more elected presidents?

5. Who was the first American to be awarded the Nobel Peace Prize?

6. Who is the only president buried in Washington, D.C.?

7. Before it stood for "Grand Old Party," what did the acronym GOP stand for?

8. Which Republican vice presidents took over the presidency?

9. Which Republican president had a Democrat as his vice president?

10. Who invented the famous elephant symbol that continues to represent the Republican Party?

1. Abraham Lincoln was elected president in the election of 1860.
2. Ronald Reagan was elected president of the Screen Actors Guild in 1947 and was reelected to five additional one-year terms.
3. Four: Abraham Lincoln, James Garfield, William McKinley, Warren G. Harding
4. The Republicans have 17 while the Democrats have 14. However, if you include the four presidents who were elected as Democrat-Republicans (the party that later became the Democrat Party), then the Democrats have more elected presidents, by one.
5. Theodore Roosevelt, in 1906, for his peacemaking role in the Russo-Japanese War.
6. Woodrow Wilson is buried in the Washington National Cathedral.
7. The acronym dates back to 1875 and originally stood for "Gallant Old Party."
8. Chester Arthur assumed the presidency after James Garfield was assassinated in 1881; Theodore Roosevelt became president after William McKinley was assassinated in 1901; Calvin Coolidge took over the presidency after Warren Harding died of a heart attack in 1923; Gerald Ford became Commander-in-Chief after Richard Nixon resigned in 1974.
9. Abraham Lincoln's vice president was Southerner and Democrat Andrew Johnson. Arguing that their National Union Party was for all loyal men, the Republicans extended Johnson's nomination in 1864.
10. Cartoonist Thomas Nast first drew the now-famous elephant in a cartoon for Harper's Weekly in 1874.

Politically Conscious Kid

M_y first foray into politics came long before I cast my first vote. In 1936, I was in the fourth grade, but that was the year I first discovered not every family thinks alike. Both my parents were staunch, second-generation Republicans. My dad, a white-collar worker in the automobile industry, spent his days expediting orders and tracking down shipments, while my best friend's dad was a pro-union tool and dye maker, and a steadfast Democrat.

Unlike today's campaigns that grow ever longer with each election, back then the presidential campaign commenced about the same time the school fall semester began—the day after Labor Day. For the next six weeks, my friend and I spent much of our daily walks to and from school arguing about our parents' political convictions.

"My dad says Roosevelt wants too much power, and so do the unions," I told my friend.

"Hah! If it wasn't for the unions, my dad says he wouldn't have a job," she would counter.

And so it went, neither of us swaying the other but savoring the friendly arguments. The week before the election, we arrived at our classroom to find the door blocked by the class wise guy. "Roosevelt or Landon?" he asked everyone, barring the door with both arms.

"Roosevelt," my friend said.

He stepped aside to let her pass.

It was my turn next. "Well, which is it?" he demanded.

I paused for a moment, hid both hands behind my back, and crossed my fingers. "Roosevelt," I replied as I pushed him aside and joined the others who had given the right answer.

Although the teacher soon put a stop to his game, we all learned the value of a secret ballot when she took advantage of our interest in political doings by holding a straw vote. Despite what we had said at the door, the result was one vote short of a tie.

Looking back, I think that was the beginning of what for me evolved into a lifetime interest in politics. Young as I was, it made me realize that people can be friends even if they don't think alike, and that we are all entitled to our own beliefs

I never again hedged about my political preference, although as a first-time voter, I did toy with the idea of registering Democrat. That would really show my family I had a mind of my own. I didn't do it, though.

Years later I did shake up my father-in-law. Like my childhood friend's father, he was a union man and a dyed-in-the-wool Democrat. In 1956, we were sitting around the table after Thanksgiving dinner when talk turned toward Eisenhower's reelection.

"You didn't vote for him, did you?" my father-in-law asked, looking aghast at first my husband, then me.

If only I had a picture of the expression on his face when I smiled and said, "Of course we did."

Marilyn Jensen

Confessions of a Black Conservative

A urine smell permeated the stair-well. Because of smashed light bulbs, I walked in darkness; the crunch of broken wine bottles underfoot echoed off the concrete walls. With the elevators out of service half of the time due to vandalism, I was forced to take the scary trek into the shadow of death up the stairwell to our sixth-floor apartment in the projects of East Baltimore. I was nine years old.

This current condition was a far cry from the brand-spanking-new building we had moved into just two years earlier. I remember our excitement when my parents, three younger siblings, and I moved into our apartment. Moving from our leaky-roof ghetto habitat into a place where everything was new, including the appliances, was a dream come true. We were one of the first in the eleven-story all-black residents building. Although a few people kept their apartments lovely, most seemed committed to destroying the building.

I kept hearing that everything was the "white man's fault." Even at age nine, I sarcastically thought to myself, "How can we stop these evil white people from sneaking in here at night, peeing in the stairwell, leaving broken wine bottles, smashing the light bulbs, and attacking people?"

My early experience living in the government project taught me that some folks simply have a ghetto mindset. I also witnessed the trap of government welfare. And why were so many around me angry and violent despite getting free housing, food, and health care?

It was the late '50s when my dad became one of the first blacks to break the color barrier in the Baltimore Fire Department. The sight of him in his crisp, dress blue firefighter uniform made everyone proud, though none more than me. With dad's new job, the government raised our rent to $72 per month. I remember my dad saying, "Seventy-two dollars! They must be crazy. We're movin'!" We moved to a suburban black community. I truly believe I would not be who I am today had we stayed in the projects.

Several of my cousins stayed enslaved to the system and the bigotry of low expectations. Because true self-esteem comes from personal achievement, they possessed very little. They lived angry and bitter lives consumed with serial impregnating, out of wedlock births, and substance abuse. An outrageously high number died prematurely.

So when I hear politicians pandering to the so-called poor of America, it turns my stomach. I've witnessed the deterioration of the human spirit, wasted lives, and suffering that happens when government becomes "daddy."

Lloyd Marcus

Party Animal

The motley crowd sported frayed denims and grubby tennies, crisp corduroys and snow boots, even suits and ties. I selected a sugar cookie from the trays lining a table and elbowed my husband as we stood in line at the caucus.

"No wonder they call us a 'party!'" Someone in the packed hallway jostled my hot chocolate, and I steadied the mug to keep it from sloshing. "Wow! Look what we've been missing all these years. Who knew?"

Who knew, indeed?

A super-sized Super Tuesday, the media would dub our 2008 Colorado caucuses later that night. But to this politically negligent newbie it was a surprising opportunity to greet otherwise obscure neighbors, nodding acquaintances, and old friends.

After the long wait at check-in, I took a seat.

"How many are experiencing a caucus for the first time?" the chairman asked. As hands flew into the air, he chuckled. "This is a far cry from the five attendees we usually average."

"So, why tonight, uh . . ." I scanned the nametag on the middle-aged woman sitting next to me, ". . . Alice? What finally brought you 'out of the closet' this year?"

Her arched brows settled into a furrow as she considered my question. "I want my opinion to count. And, well, our nest is empty now, and I have more time to concentrate on politics and the things that matter and—it's simply time."

Republican's Soul

Alice cocked her head at me. "I saw your hand go up, too. So, why are you here?"

I chewed the last bite of cookie as I thought about my answer.

Why was I here? In my younger decades, I'd avoided politics like a contagious disease. Busy raising a gaggle of kids, I always thought my attention had loftier objectives, more pressing directions.

Oh, don't get me wrong. During all those parenting years, I read the headlines; I listened to the news. More important, I voted. Sometimes grudgingly, I admit and—granted—most often by simply smoothing the fold lines in the sample ballot my husband had prefilled and copying his choices line for line.

"Like using a crib sheet during a college exam," he once accused.

"But at least I don't cancel out your votes," I justified. Even so, guilt dogged my footsteps like a whiny toddler each time I entered the voting booth.

So, why this year? Why my sudden interest in the electoral process?

My reasons, I knew, somewhat mirrored Alice's. It was, quite simply, time. It was time to make my opinion count, time to learn about the complexities of the political arena, and time to be involved.

But before I could frame my thoughts to respond to Alice, the chairman directed everyone to gather in the gymnasium.

After the pledge and a prayer, precinct captains rallied supporters from the crowd crammed against the stage and backed against the windows. The gym rang with opinions and spontaneous pockets of applause as we debated candidates, discussed issues, and swayed voters.

More than once during the energetic evening, I felt a fervent urge to voice my opinions. No one was more startled than I (unless it was my husband) to discover such hidden thoughts and previously unexpressed views distilled, I suppose, from years of absorbing information.

After a show of hands for the Presidential Preference Poll, our precinct agenda focused on the need for hot shot volunteers, committee members, convention delegates, alternates, and election judges. The chairman entertained nominations—and volunteers.

Energized by the faith, hope, and enthusiasm pulsing through the room, I felt a growl of hunger in the back of my throat. The opportunity was ripe. More important, so was I.

My hand shot into the air. For me it was, quite simply, time to be involved.

I was ready to "party"!

Carol McAdoo Rehme

WHSAID IT?

"Keep your eyes on the stars, and your feet on the ground."

—*Theodore Roosevelt*

"No one has deputized America to play Wyatt Earp to the world."

—*Pat Buchanan*

"Mostly I am sorry for the way I thought of other people. Like a good general, I had treated everyone who wasn't with me as against me."

—*Lee Atwater*

When you confront a problem, you begin to solve it."

—*Rudy Giuliani*

"Let us begin by committing ourselves to the truth—to see it like it is, and tell it like it is—to find the truth, to speak the truth, and to live the truth."

—*Richard Nixon*

"America is too great for small dreams."

—*Ronald Reagan*

"Everything I have, my career, my family, I owe to America."

—*Arnold Schwarzenegger*

"The nation which forgets its defenders will be itself forgotten."

—*Calvin Coolidge*

Newt Gingrich
Inaugural Address Opening of the 1995 Congress,
Delivered January 4, 1995

Let me say first of all that I am very deeply grateful to my good friend, Dick Gephardt. I couldn't help but—when my side maybe overreacted to your statement ending 40 years of Democratic rule—that I couldn't help but look over at Bob Michel, who has often been up here and who knows that everything Dick said was true—that this is difficult and painful to lose, and on my side of the aisle, we have for 20 elections been on the losing side.

And yet there is something so wonderful about the process by which a free people decides things—that, in my own case, I lost two elections, and with the good help of my friend Vic Fazio, came close to losing two others. And I'm sorry, guys; it just didn't quite work out. And yet I can tell you that every time when the polls closed and I waited for the votes to come in, I felt good, because win or lose, we've been part of this process. In a little while, I'm going to ask the dean of the House, John Dingell, to swear me in, to insist on the bipartisan nature of the way in which we together work in this House. John's father was one of the great stalwarts of the New Deal, a man who, as an FDR Democrat, created modern America. And I think that John and his father represent a tradition that we all have to recognize and respect, and recognize that the America we are now going to try to lead grew from that tradition and is part of that great heritage.

I also want to take just a moment to thank Speaker Foley, who was extraordinarily generous, both in his public utterances and in everything that he and Mrs. Foley did to help Marianne and me, and to help our staff make the transition. I think that he worked very hard to reestablish the dignity of the House. And I think that we can all be proud of the reputation that he takes and of the spirit with which he led the speakership. And our best wishes go to Speaker and Mrs. Foley.

I also want to thank the various House officers, who have been just extraordinary. And I want to say for the public record that faced with a result none of them wanted, in a situation I suspect none of them expected, but within 48 hours every officer of this House reacted as a patriot, worked overtime, bent over backwards, and in every way helped us. And I am very grateful, and this House I think owes a debt of gratitude to every officer that the Democrats elected two years ago. Thank you.

This is a historic moment. I was asked over and over, how did it feel, and the only word that comes close to adequate is "overwhelming." I feel overwhelmed in every way, overwhelmed by all the Georgians who came up, overwhelmed by my extended family that is here, overwhelmed by the historic moment. I walked out and stood on the balcony just outside the Speaker's office, looking down the Mall this morning, very early. And I was just overwhelmed by the view. I had a strong sense of being part of America and this great tradition.

I have two gavels, actually. Dick happened to use one that—maybe this was appropriate. This is a Georgia gavel I just got this morning, done by Dorsey Newman of Tallapoosa, who decided that the gavels he saw on TV weren't big enough or strong enough, so he cut down a walnut tree in his backyard, made a gavel, put a commemorative item [on it] and sent it up here. So this is a genuine Georgia gavel. I'm the first Georgia Speaker in over a hundred years. The last one, by the way, had a weird accent, too. Speaker Crisp was born in Britain.

His parents were actors and they came to the U.S.—a good word, by the way, for the value we get from immigration.

And secondly, this is the gavel that Speaker Martin used. Now I'm not sure what it says about the inflation of Government, if you put them side by side, but this was the gavel used by the last Republican Speaker. And—And I want to comment for a minute on two men who served as my leader, and from whom I learned so much and who are here today.

When I arrived as a freshman, the Republican Party, deeply dispirited by Watergate and by the loss of the Presidency, banded together and worked with a leader who helped pave the way for our great Party victory of 1980, and a man who just did a marvelous job. And I can't speak too highly of what I learned about integrity and leadership and courage from serving with him in my freshman term. And he's here with us again today. Hope all of you will recognize Congressman John Rhodes of Arizona. Let me say also that at our request, he wasn't sure he should be here at all, and then he thought he was going to hide in the back of the room. And then I insisted that he come down front, somebody who I regard as a mentor. I think virtually every Democrat in the House will say is a man who genuinely cares about and loves the House and who represents the best spirit of the House, a man who I've under and who I hope as Speaker I can always rely on for advice; and who I hope frankly I can emulate in his commitment to this institution and in his willingness to try to reach beyond his personal interest and his personal partisanship. I hope all of you will join me in thanking for his years of service, Congressman Bob Michel of Illinois.

I'm—I'm very fortunate today. I have my Mom and my Dad here. They're right up there—Bob and Kit Gingrich. And I am so delighted that they were both able to be here. You know, sometimes when you get to my age, you can't have everyone near you you'd like to. I can't say how much I learned from my Dad and his years of serving the U.S. Army and how much I learned from my Mother, who is clearly my most enthusiastic cheerleader. My daughters are here up there [in the gallery]—Kathy Love with and her husband Paul, and Jackie and her husband Mark Zyler. And the person who clearly is my closest friend and my best adviser and who, if I listened to about 20 percent more, I'd get in less trouble, my wife Marianne, is there.

I have a very large extended family between Marianne and me. And they're virtually all in town, and we've done our part for the Washington tourist season. But I couldn't help—'cause when I first came on the floor earlier, I went around and saw a number of the young people who are here—a number of the children who are on the floor, the young adults, who are close to 12 years of age. And I couldn't help but think that sitting in the back rail near the center of...the House is my—one of my nephews, Kevin McPherson, who is five; and Susan Brown, who is six; and Emily Brown, who is eight; and Laura McPherson, who is nine. And they're all back there—I think probably more than allowed to bring on, but they're my nieces and my nephew. And I have two other nephews who are a little older who are actually up in the gallery.

I couldn't help but think, as a way I wanted to start the Speakership and to talk with every member, that in a sense these young people you see around you are really what, at its best, this is all about. It is much more than the negative advertising, and the interest groups, and all the different things that make politics all too often cynical and nasty and sometimes frankly just plain miserable. What makes politics worthwhile is that the choice, as Dick Gephardt said, between what we see so tragically on the evening news and the way we try to do it is to work very hard to make this system of free, representative self-government work.

And the ultimate reason for doing that is these children, and the country they will inherit, and the world they will live in. I—we're starting the 104th Congress. I don't know if you've ever thought about the concept, but for 208 years, we gather together—the most diverse country in the history of the world. We send all sorts of people. Each of us could find at least one Member we thought was weird. And I'll tell you, if you went around the room the person chosen to be weird would be different for virtually every one of us, because we do allow and insist upon the right of a free people to send an extraordinary diversity of people here.

Brian Lamb of C-SPAN read to me Friday a phrase from de Tocqueville that was so central to the House. I've been reading Remini's biography of Henry Clay. And Henry Clay always preferred the House. He was the first strong Speaker. And he preferred the House to the Senate, although he served in both. Well he said the House is more vital, more active, more dynamic and more common.

And this is what de Tocqueville wrote (quote):

"Often there is not a distinguished man in the whole number. Its members are almost all obscure individuals whose names bring no associations to mind. They are mostly village lawyers, men in trade, or even persons belonging to the lower classes of society."

Now, if you put women in with men, I don't know that we'd change much.

But the word "vulgar" in de Tocqueville's time had a very particular meaning. And it's a meaning the world would do well to study in this room. You see, de Tocqueville was an aristocrat. He lived in a world of kings and princes. And the folks who come here come here by the one single act that their citizens freely chose them.

And I don't care what your ethnic background—what your ideology. I don't care whether you're younger or older. I don't care whether you were born in America or you're a naturalized citizen. Every one of the 435 people have equal standing because their citizens freely sent them, and their voice should be heard, and they should have a right to participate. And it is the most marvelous act of a complex, giant country trying to argue and talk—and, as Dick [Gephardt] said, to have a great debate, to reach great decisions, not through a civil war, not by bombing one of our regional capitals, not by killing a half million people, not by having snipers—and let me say unequivocally I condemn all acts of violence against the law by all people for all reasons. This is a society of law and a society of civil behavior.

Here we are as commoners together, to some extent Democrats and Republicans, to some extent liberals and conservatives, but Americans all. Steve Gunderson today gave me a copy of the "Portable Abraham Lincoln." He suggested there is much for me to learn about our party, but I would also say that it does not hurt to have a copy of the portable F.D.R. This is a great country of great people. If there is any one factor or acts of my life that strikes me as I stand up here as the first Republican in 40 years to do so. When I first became whip in 1989, Russia was beginning to change, the Soviet Union as it was then. Into my whip's office one day came eight Russians and a Lithuanian, members of the Communist Party, newspaper editors. They asked me, "What does a whip do?" They said, "In Russia we have never had a free parliament since 1917 and that was only for a few months, so what do you do?" I tried to explain, as Dave Bonior or Tom DeLay might now. It is a little strange if you are from a dictatorship to explain you are called the whip but you do not really have a whip, you are elected by the people you are supposed to pressure—other members. If you pressure them too much they will not reelect you. On the other hand if you do not pressure them enough they will not reelect you.

Democracy is hard. It is frustrating. So our group came into the Chamber. The Lithuanian was a man in his late sixties, and I allowed him to come up here and sit and be Speaker, something many of us have done with constituents. Remember, this is the very beginning of perestroika and glasnost. When he came out of the chair, he was physically trembling. He was almost in tears. He said, "Ever since World War II, I have remembered what the Americans did and I have never believed the propaganda. But I have to tell you, I did not think in my life that I would be able to sit at the center of freedom." It was one of the most overwhelming, compelling moments of my life. It struck me that something I could not help but think of when we were here with President Mandela. I went over and saw Ron Dellums and thought of the great work Ron had done to extend freedom across the planet. You get that sense of emotion when you see something so totally different than you had expected. Here was a man who reminded me first of all that while presidents are important, they are in effect an elected kingship that this and the other body across the way are where freedom has to be fought out. That is the tradition I hope that we will take with us as we go to work.

Today we had a bipartisan prayer service. Frank Wolf made some very important points. He said, "We have to recognize that many of our most painful problems as a country are moral problems, problems of dealing with ourselves and with life." He said character is the key to leadership and we have to deal with that. He preached a little bit. I do not think he thought he was preaching, but he was. It was about a spirit of reconciliation. He talked about caring about our spouses and our children and our families. If we are not prepared to model our own family life beyond just having them here for 1 day, if we are not prepared to care about our children and we are not prepared to care about our families, then by what arrogance do we think we will transcend our behavior to care about others?

That is why with Congressman Gephardt's help we have established a bipartisan task force on the family. We have established the principle that we are going to set schedules we stick to so families can count on time to be together, built around school schedules so that families can get to know each other, and not just by seeing us on C-SPAN. I will also say that means one of the strongest recommendations of the bipartisan committee, is that we have 17 minutes to vote. This is the bipartisan committee's recommendations, not just mine. They pointed out that if we take the time we spent in the last Congress where we waited for one more Member, and one more, and one more, that we literally can shorten the business and get people home if we will be strict and firm. At one point this year we had a 45-minute vote. I hope all of my colleagues are paying attention because we are in fact going to work very hard to have 17 minute votes and it is over.

So, leave on the first bell, not the second bell. Okay?

This may seem particularly inappropriate to say on the first day because this will be the busiest day on opening day in congressional history. I want to read just a part of the Contract with America. I don't mean this as a partisan act, but rather to remind all of us what we are about to go through and why. Those of us who ended up in the majority stood on these steps and signed a contract, and here is part of what it says: On the first day of the 104th Congress the new Republican majority will immediately pass the following reforms aimed at restoring the faith and trust of the American people in their government:

- First, require all laws that apply to the rest of the country also to apply equally to the Congress.

- Second, select a major, independent auditing firm to conduct a comprehensive audit of the Congress for waste, fraud or abuse.
- Third, cut the number of House committees and cut committee staffs by a third.
- Fourth, limit the terms of all committee chairs.
- Fifth, ban the casting of proxy votes in committees.
- Sixth, require committee meetings to be open to the public.
- Seven, require a three-fifths majority vote to pass a tax increase.
- Eight, guarantee an honest accounting of our federal budget by implementing zero baseline budgeting.

Now, I told Dick Gephardt last night that if I had to do it over again we would have pledged within three days that we will do these things, but that is not what we said. So we have ourselves in a little bit of a box here.

Then we go a step further. I carry the TV Guide version of the contract with me at all times. We then say that within the first 100 days of the 104th Congress we shall bring to the House floor the following bills, each to be given full and open debate, each to be given a full and clear vote, and each to be immediately available for inspection. We made it available that day. We listed 10 items.

- A balanced budget amendment and line-item veto,
- A bill to stop violent criminals, emphasizing among other things an effective and enforceable death penalty.
- Third was welfare reform.
- Fourth, legislation protecting our kids.
- Fifth was to provide tax cuts for families.
- Sixth was a bill to strengthen our national defense.

- Seventh was a bill to raise the senior citizens' earning limit.
- Eighth was legislation rolling back Government regulations.
- Ninth was a commonsense legal reform bill, and
- tenth was a congressional term limits legislation.

Our commitment on our side, and this is an absolute obligation, is first of all to work today until we are done. I know that is going to inconvenience people who have families and supporters. But we were hired to do a job, and we have to start today to prove we will do it. Second, I would say to our friends in the Democratic Party that we are going to work with you, and we are really laying out a schedule working with the minority leader to make sure that we can set dates certain to go home. That does mean that if 2 or 3 weeks out we are running short we will, frankly, have longer sessions on Tuesday, Wednesday, and Thursday. We will try to work this out on a bipartisan basis to, in a workmanlike way, get it done. It is going to mean the busiest early months since 1933.

Beyond the Contract I think there are two giant challenges. I know I am a partisan figure. But I really hope today that I can speak for a minute to my friends in the Democratic Party as well as my own colleagues, and speak to the country about these two challenges so that I hope we can have a real dialog.

One challenge is to achieve a balanced budget by 2002. I think both Democratic and Republican Governors will say we can do that but it is hard. I do not think we can do it in a year or two. I do not think we ought to lie to the American people. This is a huge, complicated job.

The second challenge is to find a way to truly replace the current welfare state with an opportunity society. Let me talk very briefly about both challenges. First, on the balanced budget I think we can get it done. I think the baby boomers are now old enough that we can have an honest dialog about priorities, about resources, about what works, and what does not work. Let me say I have already told Vice President Gore that we are going to invite him to address a Republican conference. We would have invited him in December but he had to go to Moscow, I believe there are grounds for us to talk together and to work together, to have hearings together, and to have task forces together.

If we set priorities, if we apply the principles of Edwards, Deming and of Peter Drucker we can build on the Vice President's reinventing government effort and we can focus on transforming, not just cutting. The choice becomes not just do you want more or do you want less, but are there ways to do it better? Can we learn from the private sector, can we learn from Ford, IBM, from Microsoft, from what General Motors has had to go through? I think on a bipartisan basis we owe it to our children and grandchildren to get this Government in order and to be able to actually pay our way. I think 2002 is a reasonable time frame. I would hope that together we could open a dialog with the American people.

I have said that I think Social Security ought to be off limits, at least for the first 4 to 6 years of the process, because I think it will just destroy us if we try to bring it into the game. But let me say about everything else, whether it is Medicare, or it is agricultural subsidies, or it is defense or anything that I think the greatest Democratic President of the 20th century, and in my judgment the greatest President of the 20th century, said it right.

On March 4, 1933, he stood in braces as a man who had polio at a time when nobody who had that kind of disability could be anything in public life. He was President of the United States, and he stood in front of this Capitol on a rainy March day and he said, `We have nothing to fear but fear itself.` I want every one of us to reach out in that spirit and pledge to live up to that spirit, and I think frankly on a bipartisan basis. I would say to Members of the Black and Hispanic Caucuses that I would hope we could arrange by late spring to genuinely share districts.

You could have a Republican who frankly may not know a thing about your district agree to come for a long weekend with you, and you will agree to go for a long weekend with them. We begin a dialog and an openness that is totally different than people are used to seeing in politics in America. I believe if we do that we can then create a dialog that can lead to a balanced budget. But I think we have a greater challenge. I do want to pick up directly on what Dick Gephardt said, because he said it right. No Republican here should kid themselves about it. The greatest leaders in fighting for an integrated America in the 20th century were in the Democratic Party. The fact is that it was the liberal wing of the Democratic Party that ended segregation. The fact is that it was Franklin Delano Roosevelt who gave hope to a Nation that was in distress and could have slid into dictatorship. Every Republican has much to learn from studying what the Democrats did right.

But I would say to my friends in the Democratic Party that there is much to what Ronald Reagan was trying to get done. There's much to what is being done today by Republicans like Bill Weld, and John Engler, and Tommy Thompson, and George Allen, and Christy Whitman, and Pete Wilson. There is much we can share with each other.

We must replace the welfare state with an opportunity society. The balanced budget is the right thing to do. But it does not in my mind have the moral urgency of coming to grips with what is happening to the poorest Americans. I commend to all Marvin Olasky's "The Tragedy of American Compassion." Olasky goes back for 300 years and looked at what has worked in America, how we have helped people rise beyond poverty, and how we have reached out to save people. He may not have the answers, but he has the right sense of where we have to go as Americans. I do not believe that there is a single American who can see a news report of a 4-year-old thrown off of a public housing project in Chicago by other children and killed and not feel that a part of your heart went, too.

I think of my nephew in the back, Kevin, and how all of us feel about our children. How can any American read about an eleven-year-old buried with his Teddy bear because he killed a fourteen-year-old, and then another fourteen-year-old killed him, and not have some sense of "My God, where has this country gone?" How can we not decide that this is a moral crisis equal to segregation, equal to slavery? How can we not insist that every day we take steps to do something? I have seldom been more shaken than I was after the election when I had breakfast with two members of the Black Caucus. One of them said to me, "Can you imagine what it is like to visit a first-grade class and realize that every fourth or fifth young boy in that class may be dead or in jail within 15 years? And they are your constituents and you are helpless to change it?"

For some reason, I do not know why, maybe because I visit a lot of schools that got through. I mean, that personalized it. That made it real, not just statistics, but real people. Then I tried to explain part of my thoughts by talking about the need for alternatives to the bureaucracy, and we got into what I think frankly has been a pretty distorted and cheap debate over orphanages. Let me say, first of all, my father, who is here today, was a foster child. He was adopted as a teenager. I am adopted. We have relatives who were adopted. We are not talking out of some vague impersonal Dickens "Bleak House" middle-class intellectual model. We have lived the alternatives. I believe when we are told that children are so lost in the city bureaucracies that there are children who end up in dumpsters, when we are told that there are children doomed to go to schools where 70 or 80 percent of them will not graduate, when we are told of public housing projects that are so dangerous that if any private sector ran them they would be put in jail, and the only solution we are given is, `Well, we will study it, we will get around to it,` my only point is that this is unacceptable.

We can find ways immediately to do things better, to reach out, break through the bureaucracy and give every young American child a better chance. Let me suggest to you Morris Schectman's new book. I do not agree with all of it, but it is fascinating. It is entitled "Working Without a Net." It is an effort to argue that in the 21st century we have to create our own safety nets. He draws a distinction between caring and caretaking. It is worth every American reading. He said caretaking is when you bother me a little bit, and I do enough, I feel better because I think I took care of you. That is not any good to you at all. You may be in fact an alcoholic and I just gave you the money to buy the bottle that kills you, but I feel better and go home. He said caring is actually stopping and dealing with the human being, trying to understand enough about them to genuinely make sure you improve their life, even if you have to start with a conversation like, "If you will quit drinking, I will help you get a job." This is a lot harder conversation than, "I feel better. I gave him a buck or 5 bucks."

I want to commend every Member on both sides to look carefully. I say to those Republicans who believe in total privatization, you cannot believe in the Good Samaritan and explain that as long as business is making money we can walk by a fellow American who is hurt and not do something. I would say to my friends on the left who believe there has never been a government program that was not worth keeping, you cannot look at some of the results we now have and not want to reach out to the humans and forget the bureaucracies. If we could build that attitude on both sides of this aisle, we would be an amazingly different place, and the country would begin to be a different place. We have to create a partnership. We have to reach out to the American people. We are going to do a lot of important things.

Thanks to the House Information System and Congressman Vern Ehlers, as of today we are going to be on line for the whole country, every amendment, every conference report. We are working with C-SPAN and others, and Congressman Gephardt has agreed to help on a bipartisan basis to make the building more open to television, more accessible to the American people. We have talk radio hosts here today for the first time. I hope to have a bipartisan effort to make the place accessible for all talk radio hosts of all backgrounds, no matter their ideology. The House Historian's office is going to be more aggressively run on a bipartisan basis to reach out to Close Up, and to other groups to teach what the legislative struggle is about. I think over time we can and will this spring rethink campaign reform and lobbying reform and review all ethics, including the gift rule.

But that isn't enough. Our challenge shouldn't be just to balance the budget or to pass the Contract. Our challenge should not be anything that is just legislative. We are supposed to, each one of us, be leaders. I think our challenge has to be to set as our goal, and maybe we are not going to get there in 2 years. This ought to be the goal that we go home and we tell people we believe in: that there will be a Monday morning when for the entire weekend not a single child was killed anywhere in America; that there will be a Monday morning when every child in the country went to a school that they and their parents thought prepared them as citizens and prepared them to compete in the world market; that there will be a Monday morning where it was easy to find a job or create a job, and your own Government did not punish you if you tried. We should not be happy just with the language of politicians and the language of legislation.

We should insist that our success for America is felt in the neighborhoods, in the communities, by real people living real lives who can say, "Yes, we are safer, we are healthier, we are better educated, and America succeeds." This morning's closing hymn at the prayer service was the Battle Hymn of the Republic. It is hard to be in this building, look down past Grant to the Lincoln Memorial and not realize how painful and how difficult that battle hymn is. The key phrase is, "As he died to make men holy, let us live to make men free."

It is not just political freedom, although I agree with everything Congressman Gephardt said earlier. If you cannot afford to leave the public housing project, you are not free. If you do not know how to find a job and do not know how to create a job, you are not free. If you cannot find a place that will educate you, you are not free. If you are afraid to walk to the store because you could get killed, you are not free. So as all of us over the coming months sing that song, "As he died to make men holy, let us live to make men free."

I want us to dedicate ourselves to reach out in a genuinely non-partisan way to be honest with each other. I promise each of you that without regard to party my door is going to be open. I will listen to each of you. I will try to work with each of you. I will put in long hours, and I will guarantee that I will listen to you first. I will let you get it all out before I give you my version, because you have been patient with me today, and you have given me a chance to set the stage. But I want to close by reminding all of us of how much bigger this is than us. Because beyond talking with the American people, beyond working together, I think we can only be successful if we start with our limits.

I was very struck this morning with something Bill Emerson used, a very famous quote of Benjamin Franklin, at the point where the Constitutional Convention was deadlocked. People were tired, and there was a real possibility that the Convention was going to break up. Franklin, who was quite old and had been relatively quiet for the entire Convention, suddenly stood up and was angry, and he said: "I have lived, sir, a long time, and the longer I live the more convincing proofs I see of this truth, that God governs in the affairs of men, and if a sparrow cannot fall to the ground without His notice, is it possible that an empire can rise without His aid?" At that point the Constitutional Convention stopped. They took a day off for fasting and prayer. Then, having stopped and come together, they went back, and they solved the great question of large and small States. They wrote the Constitution, and the United States was created.

All I can do is pledge to you that, if each of us will reach out prayerfully and try to genuinely understand each other, if we will recognize that in this building we symbolize America, and that we have an obligation to talk with each other, then I think a year from now we can look on the 104th Congress as a truly amazing institution without regard to party, without regard to ideology. We can say, "Here America comes to work, and here we are preparing for those children a better future." Thank you. Good luck and God bless you.

A great moment in Republican history: U.S. President George W. Bush speaks to rescue workers, firefighters, and police officers from the rubble of Ground Zero on September 14, 2001, in New York City. Standing with Bush is retired firefighter Bob Beckwith. At right is New York Governor George Pataki.

Trivia

1. What was "waving the bloody shirt"?

2. What Republican campaign promised "two chickens in every pot and a car in every garage"?

3. Who referred to the "silent majority"?

4. Who was the first sitting United States Senator to be elected president?

5. Who was the tallest president?

6. Who was the first president to appear in all fifty states?

7. Who was the first president to leave the country while in office?

8. Which president weighed the most?

9. Which president started the tradition of throwing out the "first pitch" of the baseball season?

10. Who was the first president to ride in a submarine and in an airplane?

1. The term refers to a scene in William Shakespeare's play Julius Caesar, when Mark Antony displays Caesar's bloody toga at his funeral to rouse the people. In the late nineteenth century, Republican orators reminded voters that the Democratic Party was associated with slavery and secession.

2. That of Herbert Hoover in 1928

3. Richard M. Nixon in 1969

4. Warren G. Harding in 1920

5. Abraham Lincoln at 6 feet 4 inches

6. Richard M. Nixon

7. Theodore Roosevelt, who visited the Panama Canal worksite in 1906

8. William Howard Taft, at 300 pounds

9. William Howard Taft, April 4, 1910

10. Theodore Roosevelt, who rode in a submarine in 1905 and an airplane in 1910

Bent Heads, Elevated Knees

"Shh!" teacher commanded. But we elementary school children, sitting in the hallway with arms above our bent heads and our knees elevated, couldn't help but let our giggles escape.

It was a World War II air raid drill. No bad planes were going to spew bombs, but the teachers said we had to rehearse. Didn't they realize that *if* a bomb fell, it would crush the building with us inside?

That war found me closing blackout shades over my windows whenever a siren sounded, and my dad donned his Air Raid Warden's hat and patrolled our street in the darkness. I wore a dog tag whenever I was at school. The rectangular identification dangled from the linguine-shaped plastic chain around my neck. My fingerprints were inked on a blue cardboard. I liked looking at the swirls, which someone said were different from anyone else's, anyplace, but, of course, I didn't believe that. Were only New York schoolchildren fingerprinted and dog-tagged? I believed we were special enough for that.

Occasionally, our Long Island, New York, house was in the flight path of passing airplanes; I waved to the pilot, believing he could see me. After all, if a lit match could be seen for a hundred miles in the darkness, why would I doubt a pilot could miss my waving arms?

Ration books were interesting, short wave radio broadcasts were silly sounding, V-mail was fun to write and receive, especially when thick black lines went through the letter before being photographed and reduced in size. Jewelry covered with radium-paint was great, because I could hold it under the light, then take it into a dark closet and see it glow.

Why did my parents say, "Shh," when President Roosevelt spoke? Just another radio voice to me, and I'd rather hear singers anyway. Why did they gasp when someplace called Pearl Harbor was attacked? It was far away and had nothing to do with us. Later, when I heard the word "kamikaze," I repeated it over and over, impressed by my ability to use a "foreign" word and its singsong syllables.

I was quite patriotic and made small balls of tinfoil; I don't know where my mother took them after I rolled each, but it seemed so grown-up to be helping Uncle Sam. When I asked my teacher who Uncle Sam really was, I didn't get an answer.

I used some of my allowance for a war bond, but was unsure why a piece of paper was valuable, since I couldn't exchange it for Sugar-Dot candy, Indian nuts, or charlotte russe. My parents said that money was helping the country, and I didn't question that because they sometimes seemed preoccupied with war things. My mother was never preoccupied enough to forget the awful oily vitamin liquid she spooned into my mouth before every morning's orange juice.

Each morning, the electric space heater seemed to find its way into my bedroom first; in front of it, I warmed my socks and cotton undershirts. So, I didn't find heat lacking, although others seemed to grumble. And we already had a car we hardly used, since the Long Island Railroad's Broadway stop was only a few city blocks away, and we took the train in and out of the city, so even car gas wasn't my problem. Why did some people complain about too little of that?

Nothing bad happens in America, like the Movietone newsreels showed during intermissions of a double-feature film. Rubble, scared families, flames, noisy aircraft with bomb bay doors, and bewildered survivors were just like real Hollywood movies. Every Saturday afternoon, I got to see the weekly news on film, except that's usually when I got up to buy some more sticky candy or go to the bathroom.

Learning about donkeys and elephants in high school, I asked my parents which they were, which led to more confusion. They both said they vote for a specific person and not a party. Well, I knew they voted for Roosevelt, so I thought maybe they preferred that party.

I now have a Medicare card, and my parents share a granite headstone in a cemetery. Warlike events still happen everyplace, it seems, except in America.

September 11, 2001. Where pushcarts once peddled produce, and a telephone company building was background, two tall rectangles had been erected in the 1970s and stood with the pompous title World Trade Center towers. No bomb bay doors opened evacuating steel cylinders, but aircraft assaulted the towers, tearing them apart and eradicating humans. Washington, D.C.'s Pentagon was pierced by another aircraft. Rubble, scared families, flames, bewildered survivors were no longer Movietone black-and-white newsreels of faraway places. America was no longer safe and spared from invaders and destruction. Two of my grandsons witnessed the second explosion from their Brooklyn school's rooftop. Nothing can erase that scene for them, for Americans, for those who will forever mourn the human loss, for the complacent who thought our invisible shield could not be penetrated.

December 21, 2002. President Bush received a vaccination to prevent smallpox. Germ warfare has become a possibility. No corners exist in which to sit with bent head and elevated knees curled up as protection.

Long ago, when I registered to vote, and was asked "Party," I penned Republican, merely because I liked the sounds of the syllables. I continue to pull that lever because I've hoped that conservative strength will also show other world leaders that we have politicians who have dignity. Metal detectors, media images of horror, airline searches . . . I don't want America's leader to be my pal, or to be voted for because of racial or gender pushes on the public. I remember bent heads and elevated knees and hope the Republican Party can prevent current students from having that experience.

Lois Greene Stone

Every Vote Counts

He was honest.

He cared about the community.

He had good ideas.

Tony was my neighbor, and he was running for town council. It was 1975. I was in high school, Richard Nixon had just resigned, and the Vietnam War was coming to a close. America was changing, and my neighbor Tony was going to help make things better.

Tony was in his early thirties. He lived in the split-level ranch next door with his wife and their two small children. One of my sisters babysat for the kids. I raked their yard. Tony was excited about becoming a member of the town council. He was running against a longtime incumbent, and he wasn't supposed to have a chance. Everyone but Tony knew that he couldn't win.

I remember the night Tony announced his candidacy to my parents. We sat on my parents' back porch as Tony pleaded his case. "This town needs change," he told them. "We need to be represented." And he was right. We lived in a small, new development in rural northeastern Connecticut. The development and its residents were markedly different from the farms and Yankee farmers surrounding it. The needs of the commuting suburbanites were very different from those of the more entrenched farmers. The suburbanites required more services from the town, and the political landscape was changing.

"Do I have your vote?" Tony finally asked my mom and dad.

Without hesitation, my father answered him: "We don't vote."

Tony was flabbergasted. "Never?" he asked. "You've never voted?" They hadn't, and my dad made it clear that they weren't about to start now. Tony looked to my mother for help. She shook her head.

Over and over, Tony asked my parents why they didn't vote, and the answer was always the same: it didn't matter. They didn't believe their votes would make a difference.

Tony spent the next half-hour trying to convince my parents to register to vote. He talked about civic duty, about responsibility to the community, and about making the town better for their children. Tony talked until my parents were out of polite patience. Finally, Tony made a personal appeal.

"Will you do it for me? Will you do it just to help your neighbor?"

They politely refused. Tony finally gave up.

Tony ran a great grassroots campaign. He walked door to door and talked to everyone who would listen. He was honest, he cared about the community, and he had good ideas. With each passing day, Tony closed the gap on the longtime incumbent.

In the final days before the election, Tony tried repeatedly to convince my parents to vote. I remember him telling them, "This is going to be a very close election. I'm going to need every vote." Mom and Dad were unmoved.

You've probably figured out the end of this story. After all, it is pretty predictable. Tony lost by a single vote. Had my parents voted for him, he would have won by a single vote. Things were never the same between Tony and my parents. I never saw them speak again. About six months after the election, Tony put his house up for sale. It sold quickly, and Tony and his family moved away less than a year after the election.

My parents never considered Tony's defeat their fault. They often discussed it, but only with each other. It always seemed to me that they just couldn't admit, even to themselves, that they were wrong about their votes not counting. My parents never did register to vote. My mother passed several years ago; she lived her whole life without ever casting a vote. Dad is nearly eighty, and also has no intention of ever voting.

The incident had a lasting effect on me. I registered to vote the day I was eligible, and I've voted in every election—major and minor— since then. Even when I was in the service and far from home, I voted in every election. My sisters mailed information to me about the issues and candidates, and I cast absentee ballots. I voted in several presidential elections this way. Both of my sisters were similarly affected. They, too, vote in every election.

And the best part is that my children have learned the lesson, too. All three of my daughters vote—in every election. We live in Florida, and we were here for the Florida 2000 election debacle. My entire family—except for my youngest daughter, who was too young to vote then—voted in that election. We watched the election night results together until the wee hours of the morning. Like many others, we were greeted that Wednesday morning, after very little sleep, with the news that the election had not been decided.

I was thrilled when my youngest daughter told me: "You're right, Dad. Every vote does count!" Even though she was too young to vote in that election, she learned the same lesson I had learned twenty-five years before: even if it is cliché, every vote does count, and we all have a responsibility to vote.

By their example, my parents taught me that every vote counts, and their refusal to vote actually determined the outcome of an election. I learned by watching my parents do the wrong thing. I wanted my daughters to learn by the right example, and so I took at least one of them to the polling place every time I voted. Not only did I create fond memories of holding one of my daughters' hands while casting my vote, I also feel I helped them understand the responsibility we all have as citizens. By sharing the story of Tony's heartbreaking run for office, I gave them a real-life example of the truth in the statement that "every vote counts."

C. A. Verno

The Party of the Rich ... but Which Party?

From the time I was a young boy, I heard that "Republicans are the party of the rich." My parents were among the few Republicans in a precinct dominated by Democrats, and this allegation made my father angry. He fired a boiler at a Catholic hospital and was lower middle class. A German immigrant, he came to the United States because of the kindness of the chaplain at the Catholic hospital and a foreman at the J. I. Case tractor plant, who sponsored him and agreed to care for him for five years if needed. My father had never met the man until he arrived in America.

We were anything but rich. We did not have a car for eleven years. We never took a vacation. We didn't have many things that ordinary households had. My father was just happy to be in America. He felt he was far better off here than if he had stayed in depression-torn Germany. He became a Republican because he believed President Franklin D. Roosevelt had broken his promises. Whenever my father heard Roosevelt insist that the Republican Party consisted only of rich people, he became so upset that my mother had to calm him down.

God rest his soul, my father has been gone for twenty years now. I wish he could have seen the many things that would have brought great joy to his heart. Like the dissolution of the Soviet Union, of which he was a fierce opponent, or the study by my friend and colleague Mike Franc, Vice President for Congressional Relations at the Heritage Foundation. Using data provided by the Internal

Revenue Service, Franc looked at single-filer taxpayers earning more than $100,000 per year and married joint-filers earning more than $200,000 per year. He discovered that the Democratic Party is the "party of the rich." Franc said, "Electing Democrats is very closely correlated with how many wealthy households are in a district."

Franc said that the number of Democrats representing wealthy districts significantly increased after the 2006 elections. These Democrats have pushed for passage of H.R. 3970, the Tax Reduction and Reform Act of 2007. Proposed by House Ways and Means Committee Chairman Charles B. Rangel (D-NY), the bill would eliminate the middle class from the Alternative Minimum Tax (AMT), a tax originally intended for the very wealthy but which more and more Americans must pay each year because its income requirement was not indexed to inflation. To make up for the shortfall that would result in this loss of revenue, the bill also proposes an enormous increase in taxes for Americans whose adjusted gross incomes are in excess of $250,000. The bill probably will be dead upon arrival in the Senate. Franc said the Democrats can't go too far in levying huge tax increases on the rich because they would be doing it to themselves.

As with the surge in Iraq, the success of which key Democrats refuse to acknowledge, it is unlikely Democrats will admit they are now the party of the rich. They need to appear as the party of the poor to maintain specific voting blocs. Still, if mainstream media would acknowledge the new party of the rich just as it now acknowledges the success of the surge in Iraq, things may change. Want to guess which Republican will brand the Democrats the party of the rich?

Paul Weyrich

"Being a Democrat is hard . . . it's so taxing."

WHSAID IT?

"Peace is not made at the Council table or by treaties, but in the hearts of men."

—*Herbert Hoover*

"Avoid having your ego so close to your position that when your position falls, your ego goes with it."

—*Colin Powell*

"Politics is just like show business. You have a hell of an opening, coast for a while, and then have a hell of a close."

—*Ronald Reagan*

"Presidents come and go, but the Supreme Court goes on forever."

—*William Howard Taft*

"Happiness is like a cat. If you try to coax it or call it, it will avoid you; it will never come. But if you pay not attention to it and go about your business, you'll find it rubbing against your legs and jumping into your lap."

—*William Bennett*

"He serves his party best who serves his country best."

—*Rutherford B. Hayes*

"If anyone tells you that America's best days are behind her, they're looking the wrong way."

—*George H. W. Bush*

"When there is a lack of honor in government, the morals of the whole people are poisoned."

—*Herbert Hoover*

George W. Bush

Address to a Joint Session of Congress Following 9/11 Attacks

Delivered September 20, 2001

M r. Speaker, Mr. President Pro Tempore, members of Congress, and fellow Americans:

In the normal course of events, Presidents come to this chamber to report on the state of the Union. Tonight, no such report is needed. It has already been delivered by the American people.

We have seen it in the courage of passengers, who rushed terrorists to save others on the ground—passengers like an exceptional man named Todd Beamer. And would you please help me to welcome his wife, Lisa Beamer, here tonight. We have seen the state of our Union in the endurance of rescuers, working past exhaustion. We've seen the unfurling of flags, lighting of candles, giving of blood, saying of prayers—in English, Hebrew, and Arabic. We have seen the decency of a loving and giving people who have made the grief of strangers their own. My fellow citizens, for the last nine days, the entire world has seen for itself the state of our Union—and it is strong.

Tonight we are a country awakened to danger and called to defend freedom. Our grief has turned to anger, and anger to resolution. Whether we bring our enemies to justice, or bring justice to our enemies, justice will be done. I thank the Congress for its leadership at such an important time. All of America was touched on the evening of the tragedy to see Republicans and Democrats joined together on the steps of this Capitol, singing "God Bless America." And you did more than sing; you acted, by delivering 40 billion dollars to rebuild our communities and meet the needs of our military. Speaker Hastert, Minority Leader Gephardt, Majority Leader Daschle, and Senator Lott, I thank you for your friendship, for your leadership, and for your service to our country. And on behalf of the American people, I thank the world for its outpouring of support. America will never forget the sounds of our National Anthem playing at Buckingham Palace, on the streets of Paris, and at Berlin's Brandenburg Gate.

We will not forget South Korean children gathering to pray outside our embassy in Seoul, or the prayers of sympathy offered at a mosque in Cairo. We will not forget moments of silence and days of mourning in Australia and Africa and Latin America. Nor will we forget the citizens of 80 other nations who died with our own: dozens of Pakistanis; more than 130 Israelis; more than 250 citizens of India; men and women from El Salvador, Iran, Mexico, and Japan; and hundreds of British citizens. America has no truer friend than Great Britain. Once again, we are joined together in a great cause—so honored the British Prime Minister has crossed an ocean to show his unity with America. Thank you for coming friend.

On September the 11th, enemies of freedom committed an act of war against our country. Americans have known wars—but for the past 136 years, they have been wars on foreign soil, except for one Sunday in 1941. Americans have known the casualties of war—but not at the center of a great city on a peaceful morning. Americans have known surprise attacks—but never before on thousands of civilians. All of this was brought upon us in a single day—and night fell on a different world, a world where freedom itself is under attack. Americans have many questions tonight. Americans are asking: Who attacked our country? The evidence we have gathered all points to a collection of loosely affiliated terrorist organizations known as al Qaeda. They are some of the murderers indicted for bombing American embassies in Tanzania and Kenya, and responsible for bombing the USS Cole. Al Qaeda is to terror what the mafia is to crime. But its goal is not making money; its goal is remaking the world—and imposing its radical beliefs on people everywhere.

The terrorists practice a fringe form of Islamic extremism that has been rejected by Muslim scholars and the vast majority of Muslim clerics, a fringe movement that perverts the peaceful teachings of Islam. The terrorists' directive commands them to kill Christians and Jews, to kill all Americans, and make no distinctions among military and civilians, including women and children. This group and its leader—a person named Usama bin Laden—are linked to many other organizations in different countries, including the Egyptian Islamic Jihad and the Islamic Movement of Uzbekistan. There are thousands of these terrorists in more than 60 countries. They are recruited from their own nations and neighborhoods and brought to camps in places like Afghanistan, where they are trained in the tactics of terror. They are sent back to their homes or sent to hide in countries around the world to plot evil and destruction.

The leadership of al Qaeda has great influence in Afghanistan and supports the Taliban regime in controlling most of that country. In Afghanistan, we see al Qaeda's vision for the world. Afghanistan's people have been brutalized; many are starving and many have fled. Women are not allowed to attend school. You can be jailed for owning a television. Religion can be practiced only as their leaders dictate.

A man can be jailed in Afghanistan if his beard is not long enough.

The United States respects the people of Afghanistan. After all, we are currently its largest source of humanitarian aid; but we condemn the Taliban regime. It is not only repressing its own people, it is threatening people everywhere by sponsoring and sheltering and supplying terrorists. By aiding and abetting murder, the Taliban regime is committing murder.

And tonight, the United States of America makes the following demands on the Taliban: Deliver to United States authorities all the leaders of al Qaeda who hide in your land. Release all foreign nationals, including American citizens, you have unjustly imprisoned. Protect foreign journalists, diplomats, and aid workers in your country, close immediately and permanently every terrorist training camp in Afghanistan, and hand over every terrorist, and every person in their support structure, to appropriate authorities. Give the United States full access to terrorist training camps, so we can make sure they are no longer operating. These demands are not open to negotiation or discussion. The Taliban must act, and act immediately. They will hand over the terrorists, or they will share in their fate.

I also want to speak tonight directly to Muslims throughout the world. We respect your faith. It's practiced freely by many millions of Americans and by millions more in countries that America counts as friends. Its teachings are good and peaceful, and those who commit evil in the name of Allah blaspheme the name of Allah. The terrorists are traitors to their own faith, trying, in effect, to hijack Islam itself. The enemy of America is not our many Muslim friends; it is not our many Arab friends. Our enemy is a radical network of terrorists, and every government that supports them. Our war on terror begins with al Qaeda, but it does not end there. It will not end until every terrorist group of global reach has been found, stopped, and defeated.

Americans are asking, why do they hate us? They hate what they see right here in this chamber—a democratically elected government. Their leaders are self-appointed. They hate our freedoms—our freedom of religion, our freedom of speech, our freedom to vote and assemble and disagree with each other. They want to overthrow existing governments in many Muslim countries, such as Egypt, Saudi Arabia, and Jordan. They want to drive Israel out of the Middle East. They want to drive Christians and Jews out of vast regions of Asia and Africa. These terrorists kill not merely to end lives, but to disrupt and end a way of life. With every atrocity, they hope that America grows fearful, retreating from the world and forsaking our friends. They stand against us, because we stand in their way.

We are not deceived by their pretenses to piety. We have seen their kind before. They are the heirs of all the murderous ideologies of the 20th century. By sacrificing human life to serve their radical visions—by abandoning every value except the will to power—they follow in the path of fascism, Nazism, and totalitarianism. And they will follow that path all the way, to where it ends: in history's unmarked grave of discarded lies. Americans are asking: How will we fight and win this war? We will direct every resource at our command—every means of diplomacy, every tool of intelligence, every instrument of law enforcement, every financial influence, and every necessary weapon of war—to the disruption and to the defeat of the global terror network.

Now this war will not be like the war against Iraq a decade ago, with a decisive liberation of territory and a swift conclusion. It will not look like the air war above Kosovo two years ago, where no ground troops were used and not a single American was lost in combat. Our response involves far more than instant retaliation and isolated strikes. Americans should not expect one battle, but a lengthy campaign, unlike any other we have ever seen. It may include dramatic strikes, visible on TV, and covert operations, secret even in success. We will starve terrorists of funding, turn them one against another, and drive them from place to place, until there is no refuge or no rest. And we will pursue nations that provide aid or safe haven to terrorism. Every nation, in every region, now has a decision to make. Either you are with us, or you are with the terrorists. From this day forward, any nation that continues to harbor or support terrorism will be regarded by the United States as a hostile regime.

Our nation has been put on notice: We're not immune from attack. We will take defensive measures against terrorism to protect Americans. Today, dozens of federal departments and agencies, as well as state and local governments, have responsibilities affecting homeland security. These efforts must be coordinated at the highest level. So tonight I announce the creation of a Cabinet-level position reporting directly to me—the Office of Homeland Security. And tonight I also announce a distinguished American to lead this effort, to strengthen American security: a military veteran, an effective governor, a true patriot, a trusted friend—Pennsylvania's Tom Ridge. He will lead, oversee, and coordinate a comprehensive national strategy to safeguard our country against terrorism, and respond to any attacks that may come.

These measures are essential. But the only way to defeat terrorism as a threat to our way of life is to stop it, eliminate it, and destroy it where it grows. Many will be involved in this effort; from FBI agents to intelligence operatives to the reservists we have called to active duty.

All deserve our thanks, and all have our prayers. And tonight, a few miles from the damaged Pentagon, I have a message for our military: Be ready. I've called the Armed Forces to alert, and there is a reason. The hour is coming when America will act, and you will make us proud. This is not, however, just America's fight. And what is at stake is not just America's freedom. This is the world's fight. This is civilization's fight. This is the fight of all who believe in progress and pluralism, tolerance and freedom.

We ask every nation to join us. We will ask, and we will need, the help of police forces, intelligence services, and banking systems around the world. The United States is grateful that many nations and many international organizations have already responded with sympathy and with support— nations from Latin America, to Asia, to Africa, to Europe, to the Islamic world. Perhaps the NATO Charter reflects best the attitude of the world: An attack on one is an attack on all. The civilized world is rallying to America's side. They understand that if this terror goes unpunished, their own cities, their own citizens may be next. Terror, unanswered, can not only bring down buildings, it can threaten the stability of legitimate governments. And you know what? We're not going to allow it.

Americans are asking: What is expected of us? I ask you to live your lives, and hug your children. I know many citizens have fears tonight, and I ask you to be calm and resolute, even in the face of a continuing threat. I ask you to uphold the values of America, and remember why so many have come here. We are in a fight for our principles, and our first responsibility is to live by them. No one should be singled out for unfair treatment or unkind words because of their ethnic background or religious faith. I ask you to continue to support the victims of this tragedy with your contributions. Those who want to give can go to a central source of information, libertyunites.org, to find the names of groups providing direct help in New York, Pennsylvania, and Virginia.

The thousands of FBI agents who are now at work in this investigation may need your cooperation, and I ask you to give it. I ask for your patience, with the delays and inconveniences that may accompany tighter security; and for your patience in what will be a long struggle. I ask your continued participation and confidence in the American economy. Terrorists attacked a symbol of American prosperity. They did not touch its source. America is successful because of the hard work, and creativity, and enterprise of our people. These were the true strengths of our economy before September 11th, and they are our strengths today. And, finally, please continue praying for the victims of terror and their families, for those in uniform, and for our great country. Prayer has comforted us in sorrow, and will help strengthen us for the journey ahead.

Tonight I thank my fellow Americans for what you have already done and for what you will do. And ladies and gentlemen of the Congress, I thank you, their representatives, for what you have already done and for what we will do together. Tonight, we face new and sudden national challenges. We will come together to improve air safety, to dramatically expand the number of air marshals on domestic flights, and take new measures to prevent hijacking. We will come together to promote stability and keep our airlines flying, with direct assistance during this emergency. We will come together to give law enforcement the additional tools it needs to track down terror here at home. We will come together to strengthen our intelligence capabilities to know the plans of terrorists before they act, and to find them before they strike.

We will come together to take active steps that strengthen America's economy, and put our people back to work. Tonight we welcome two leaders who embody the extraordinary spirit of all New Yorkers: Governor George Pataki, and Mayor Rudolph Giuliani. As a symbol of America's resolve, my administration will work with Congress, and these two leaders, to show the world that we will rebuild New York City.

After all that has just passed—all the lives taken, and all the possibilities and hopes that died with them—it is natural to wonder if America's future is one of fear. Some speak of an age of terror. I know there are struggles ahead, and dangers to face. But this country will define our times, not be defined by them. As long as the United States of America is determined and strong, this will not be an age of terror; this will be an age of liberty, here and across the world.

Great harm has been done to us. We have suffered great loss. And in our grief and anger we have found our mission and our moment. Freedom and fear are at war. The advance of human freedom—the great achievement of our time, and the great hope of every time—now depends on us. Our nation, this generation will lift a dark threat of violence from our people and our future. We will rally the world to this cause by our efforts, by our courage. We will not tire, we will not falter, and we will not fail.

It is my hope that in the months and years ahead, life will return almost to normal. We'll go back to our lives and routines, and that is good. Even grief recedes with time and grace. But our resolve must not pass. Each of us will remember what happened that day, and to whom it happened. We'll remember the moment the news came— where we were and what we were doing. Some will remember an image of a fire, or a story of rescue. Some will carry memories of a face and a voice gone forever.

And I will carry this: It is the police shield of a man named George Howard, who died at the World Trade Center trying to save others. It was given to me by his mom, Arlene, as a proud memorial to her son. This is my reminder of lives that ended, and a task that does not end. I will not forget this wound to our country or those who inflicted it. I will not yield; I will not rest; I will not relent in waging this struggle for freedom and security for the American people. The course of this conflict is not known, yet its outcome is certain. Freedom and fear, justice and cruelty, have always been at war, and we know that God is not neutral between them.

Fellow citizens, we'll meet violence with patient justice—assured of the rightness of our cause, and confident of the victories to come. In all that lies before us, may God grant us wisdom, and may He watch over the United States of America. Thank you.

A great moment in Republican history: Dr. Condoleeza Rice is sworn in as the first African-American female Secretary of State, January 28, 2005.

A Presidential Pursuit

Pursuing the President of the United States like the paparazzi wasn't part of my 2002 vacation plans. When my late husband Roland and I left Arizona with our grown son Kendahl, we had only intended to visit our Iowa roots. Yet, all of my mother's teaching on patriotism kicked in when I learned that President George W. Bush was coming to the Iowa State Fair.

Soon we were among 115,463 fair goers. A few thousand of us held presidential-looking passes. Our line crept forward, but appeared to go nowhere. "Follow me," said a guide with a security badge. We got within 50 feet of the Machinery Grounds before being halted. "Wait here."

Volunteers wore "Doug Gross for GOP Governor" T-shirts wrong side out. *Hmm, same surname. That might prove to be helpful.* Believe me, I conjured up enough chutzpa to try the "my name is Effie Gross" line. It didn't help.

"Those people getting in have different colored tickets," a volunteer finally offered. "Some complimentary tickets were given to the vendors who lost business today in order for us to use this area."

As Jane Q. Public, I envied the already seated VIPs. Hundreds of hopefuls, including my husband, my son, and I, stood outside the gate in mass confusion. By then, I realized that I'd lost track of Kendahl. If ever I was going to see the President, I knew it would take an act of Congress or God. I needed to muscle my way up to the front. "Excuse me. Pardon me," I said bearing toward the gate.

Sporting dark sunglasses, Secret Service personnel brushed by with a sense of urgency. On the roof, more agents stood armed with artillery, perusing the crowd and assessing the sky.

"Can't we get in?" a lady holding a crying baby asked the next Secret Service woman to pass by.

"Just a minute," she replied, walking ahead. She whispered to a co-worked and returned. "How many seats do you need?" The young mother nodded to indicate her family of four. "Come with me."

Determined not to give up, and remembering "it's polite not to ask," I interrupted, "Excuse me? May I go, too?"

"Come with me," the agent said to *me* this time.

"May my husband come?" I pleaded.

"Where is he?"

Roland overheard. He raised his hand like a man in distress being swallowed up by the quicksand crowd. "Come," she said.

For the first time in nearly two hours, the crowd was no longer pressing in on us. In the narrow area we had entered, I paused to search for Kendahl one last time. Just in case he were videotaping us being escorted in, I waved a fully outstretched arm.

Walking hand-in-hand with Roland, I thought of a familiar passage, "Many that are first shall be last; and the last shall be first." We were being ushered to seats in the second row near the stage.

Only five other Presidents, I was told, had addressed a similar crowd in the 150 years of Iowa State Fair history, and two of them were not president at the time. I felt privileged indeed.

President Bush smiled his boyish smile, and after the applause subsided, he began by offering regrets that First Lady Laura Bush couldn't come. He told a polite joke and then recognized democratic Governor Tom Vilsack. Applause and cheers interrupted President Bush's energetic speech. Roland and I took pictures like pseudo-paparazzi and sat in disbelief that among a crowd of thousands, God had favored us for this honor.

"God bless America," concluded the President's speech, but he wasn't finished until he made the way around the fence in front of the first few rows of attendees. With the Secret Service before and behind him, he slowly began greeting patrons. Roland and I clasped our worthless tickets, quickly agreeing to have the president sign them.

After he had signed mine and started to autograph Roland's ticket, I thought, *This is the President of the United States. I should say something to him.* Without hesitation, I said, "President Bush, I pray for you every day."

He stopped, made eye contact with me, and said firmly, "Thank you." I knew he meant it.

While getting his ticket autographed, Roland, a U.S. Army veteran asked, "Mr. President, would it be okay to shake your hand?"

President Bush said, "Sir, it would be my honor." He shook Roland's hand and then continued toward his exit.

For a long moment Roland and I embraced and kissed, not caring about the crowd. We had just talked with, and touched the Commander-in-Chief. What a thrill!

When we met up with Kendahl, he apologized, "Mom, I'm sorry how this turned out, but from the bleachers I got his entire speech on video for you."

"We saw President Bush from the front row!"

"There was even an empty seat marked 'RESERVED' for you," his dad couldn't wait to add.

"It's true," I confirmed. "Look. Our tickets aren't worthless any more—-we got his autograph."

Dumbfounded, Kendahl said, "That's really neat. Let me see."

"One is for you," I offered. "We don't need two."

How could I *ever* forget such a day?

In my naiveté, equipped only with desire, faith, expectancy and persistence, the highest power in the universe blessed me with a glimpse of the highest power in the land. It was seemingly impossible, considering that there were six billion people in the world. The odds against it were gargantuan. Yet, God granted me the desires of my heart that August day in Iowa when I met President George W. Bush.

Oh yes, I was shooting pictures like a pro (Republican, that is!).

Effie-Alean Gross

Is It Tuesday Yet?

If a person wants to be somebody in this life, I doubt there is anything nicer than being a Christian first, and a Republican second. My parents and their parents were all registered Republicans, forever touting that voting is a duty, not a privilege. Although politics was not even a gleam in either of our eyes, I fell in love with the assistant registrar of our university, and as religion and politics would have it, a collective sigh emerged when our families decided the match would flourish.

My handsome twenty-seven-year-old new husband was perpetually besieged by the county fathers from the Republican Central Committee. "Ken, we're here to ask if you would consider running as our legislative district's state senator. We need a young, savvy, and dynamic personality next year."

I knew this was all that Ken needed to hear from the county's leading citizenry to jump into the race. Since he was involved with the family business, some changes would need to be made, but it wasn't a question for Ken's father, a city councilman. So we were off to the races in grand style with new duds, a working committee, and a glad hand everywhere we went. A bit shy of twenty and knowing little of local and state politics, I crammed the issues daily and kept my nonvoting age strictly under wraps.

The campaign trail was long, hot, and dusty over a four-county area—farmers and cattlemen mostly, but we, too, were cattle and business folks, and Ken understood their concerns. Meanwhile, I busied myself with printing campaign posters, buttons, and pamphlets to pass out wherever people gathered. The women's Republican clubs jumped on our bandwagon and provided listings for dinners and meeting dates of all sorts. Coordinating caucuses and banquets became my job, shaving overlaps and travel time, for there were two other Republican wannabes dogging Ken's footsteps. The primaries would not necessarily be a shoo-in.

I can tell you the exact time and place I became pregnant with our first child, for not long thereafter I began suffering with morning sickness . . . all day long. My miserable, thin little frame wanted just to go home and sit out the next few months. Although thrilled with the good news, I could see how much my darlin' was counting on me. "I need my redheaded wife to smile sweetly, shake a hearty hand, and say a few words about your own background, honey. But mostly, I need you out there working with those enthusiastic Republican gals." Oh, yes, miseries or not, he had a way with him, that boy, for despite sudden rushes to the lady's room, I stayed healthy and steadfast to my commitment.

The day came when old college friends, the gubernatorial candidate and his wife, converged upon our area with their fancy caravan to tour with us. I felt like an old frump as the photographers featured the wives on television and the front pages; Marilyn in her lovely spring frock, snow white gloves, big picture hat, and pearls, and me forcing a smile just before my lunch came up.

I felt somewhat better and more energetic as the June primaries approached. If we had holes in our campaign, neither of us could imagine where they were. We gathered with our committee and families on election night for a backyard barbeque, celebrating winning handily as the Republican nominee.

Four months remained until the election, and Ken launched final pitches to convince four counties that he was equipped and ready to commit his all. With dinners, picnics, and speaking engagements once more in place, we went at it again like two whirlwinds, often meeting in decorated V.I.P. cars at local parades. I recall wangling a rural five-and-dime out of their last red and blue crepe paper to decorate our white convertible after the chairman of the project fizzled. Feeling top-notch at last, we were wired for the best, but prepared for the worst, a working motto of sorts.

A campaign stopover brought our nation's presidential candidate "Ike" and Mamie Eisenhower to our Tri-Cities on the Columbia River for the biggest rally ever witnessed in the area. Ken was ecstatic when the general insisted all Republican hopefuls be his guest on the platform the day he dedicated a new dam. It must have been a stunning but merciful death blow for our Democrat friends, but it was to be a different story when Tuesday, November 4 rolled around.

We wasted little time kicking our 488 vote loss around the block, even though I periodically caught Ken in a pensive mood. Our biggest lesson: an overwhelming Republican victory in the primaries doesn't always mean a win at the finish line. So we fell back to Earth and traveled with our son to retrieve signs, buttons, and bumper stickers, contemplating better things for another day.

Kathe Campbell

Generation to Generation —We Are Republicans

I turned twenty-one in 1966, in time for the California gubernatorial election (in those days you couldn't vote at 18). I looked forward to my first election, but my daughter tried to put a little monkey wrench in my plans.

She decided to make her arrival just five days before I was to cast my first ballot.

It was a cold day of November 8, 1966, and I had just come home from the hospital. Having been up all night with my daughter and still in pain from my stitches, I was not going be deterred from voting for the first time. I was determined and excited to be able to exercise this right and privilege.

I entered the polling area unsure of exactly how to proceed. The only thing I knew for sure was that my vote was going to be for a Republican, Ronald Reagan. After signing my name, I got my ballot and stood in line waiting for a booth to open up.

"Hey, Sallie, aren't you due to have that baby pretty soon?" called out one of the poll workers who knew me.

"Ah, well, actually I already did, five days ago."

Glancing down at my tummy bundled up in my heavy coat she seemed embarrassed and flustered at what to say.

I decided to take the high road and let her off the hook.

"I popped her out in time to come out and vote; just got home from Daniel Freeman [Hospital] this morning." I replied jokingly.

"You serious?" she asked.

"Yup! Wouldn't miss this for the world."

Before I knew it, all the women were standing and clapping. I was awestruck.

"Hey, honey, any gal who can do that and still come out to vote deserves a 'yahoo,'" my next door neighbor replied.

I felt good all over, and it felt even better to take that black stamp in my hand and put a big X in front of my favorite guy, Ronnie.

I left the voting booth with my ballot stub, which I proudly pinned to my coat for all the world to see.

As I did, tears of pride came to my eyes. I thought of my dad and how much he loved America. He took voting very seriously and spoke in glowing terms of elections, voting, and how people who didn't vote shouldn't complain. I couldn't wait to get home and call him to let him know I had voted. We would discuss how we thought the election would go and who had the best chance to win, hopefully a Republican.

I am only a second-generation American and very much my father's daughter. He held the election process dear to his heart, being the son of a German immigrant family who worked hard to come to this country. My mother and he always voted, and many heated discussions took place around election time. These were always good-natured since my mom and dad saw pretty much eye-to-eye on most things, including how to vote. My father just loved a good political repartee. We were Republicans to the core.

My dad would love to be here to debate this upcoming election. The running mates are so diverse, the issues many and complex. He would be proud to see his great-grandson, Payton, getting ready to vote for the first time this year. Payton is a staunch Republican who carries on the heated debates my father instigated. I wish my father had lived to know this fine young man. But most of all, my dad would be very proud to know he left behind a legacy.

Sallie A. Rodman

About the Contributors

Dave Beckwith, Ph.D., *served as senior pastor for Woodbridge Community Church in Irvine, California, for nearly twenty years. He retired on December 31, 2006, but continues to speak, write, and work with churches. Previously published articles have appeared in* Moody Monthly, Marriage Partnership, the Standard, BGC World, Los Angeles Times, Orange County Register, *and other publications. Dave and his wife, Joanne, have been married for thirty-eight years and have two married children and four grandchildren.*

Shawn Black *is a military veteran with the 82nd Airborne Division and former federal agent with the U.S. Department of Homeland Security. He is a civic leader, speaker, and founder of Project Prayer Flag. He is currently serving in Iraq with the U.S. State Department. To read more of his published articles and to learn more about Shawn, please visit www.shawnblack.net.*

Kathe Campbell *lives with her mammoth donkeys, a Keeshond, and a few kitties on a Montana mountain. She is a prolific writer on Alzheimer's, and her stories are found on many e-zines. Kathe is a contributing author to the* Chicken Soup for the Soul *series, numerous anthologies, "RX for Writers," and medical journals. She can be reached at kathe@wildblue.net.*

Barbara Ann Carle *is a short story writer, poet, and lifelong Democrat. She is the mother of four and the grandmother of six. One of Barbara's short stories was recently published in* Chicken Soup for the Chocolate Lover's Soul. *She is a retired police officer who resides in Friendswood, Texas, with her husband and family.*

A former professor at St. Mary's University, **Mary Lynne Gasaway** *is currently an independent scholar and writer living on a farm in Fort Worth with her husband and young* *son. As a precinct chair in the Democratic Party, she recently was an election judge in the raucous Texas primary.*

Effie-Alean Gross *is a freelance writer working and playing in Fountain Hills, AZ. A world-traveler, she loves God and Country, respectively.*

Miriam Hill *is coauthor of* Fabulous Florida *and a frequent contributor to Chicken Soup for the Soul books. She's been published in the* Christian Science Monitor, Grit, St. Petersburg Times, *and* Poynter Online. *Miriam's manuscript received Honorable Mention for Inspirational Writing in the 75th Annual* Writer's Digest *Writing Competition.*

Georgia A. Hubley *retired after twenty years in financial management to write full-time. She's a frequent contributor to the* Chicken Soup for the Soul *series,* Christian Science Monitor, *and numerous other magazines, newspapers, and anthologies. She resides with her husband of thirty years in Henderson, Nevada. Contact her at GEOHUB@aol.com.*

As a freelance writer, **Marilyn Jensen** *especially enjoys researching and writing history. She is a retired magazine editor and newspaper columnist. Her published credits include a biographical novel,* Phyllis Wheatley, *four regional history books, short stories, and articles for both children and adults in general interest and denominational publications.*

Candace Johnson *is a writer from Weston, Florida, who specializes in narrative fiction. A recent graduate of Florida Atlantic University, Candace works as a freelance proofreader and editor. The mother of two enjoys literature and travel. She can be contacted at candie542005@yahoo.com.*

Angie Klink *is the author of the lift-the-flap children's books* Purdue Peter Finds His Hammer, *showcasing Purdue University, and* I Found U, *featuring Indiana University. She writes advertising copy, personal essays, and profiles. She has won twenty-five American Advertising Federation ADDY Awards. Angie is published in* Chicken Soup for the Sister's Soul 2 *and* Our Fathers Who Art in Heaven. *Her essay "Kindergarten Karma" won an Honorable Mention in 2007 Erma Bombeck Essay Contest. Learn more at www.angieklink.com or www.mascotsforkids.com.*

About the Contributors

Conservative by heritage and Republican by choice, **Carol McAdoo Rehme** *finds inspirational writing the perfect avenue to share life's lessons. She publishes widely in anthologies and has coauthored five gift books. A ghost writer and editor, she coauthored* Chicken Soup for the Empty Nester's Soul *(2008). To learn more about Carol, please visit www.rehme.com, or she can be reached at carol@rehme.com.*

Sallie A. Rodman *is an award-winning writer whose work has appeared in numerous* Chicken Soup for the Soul *anthologies, various magazines, and the Orange County Register. She lives with her husband Paul and Inky the cat. Sallie enjoys doing mixed art media when she isn't writing. Looking ahead to the 2008 election, she can't wait for her grandson, Payton, to vote for the first time. Republican, of course! Reach her at sa.rodman@verizon.net.*

John E. Schlimm II *is an author, educator, and artist. He has served in the White House, as a publicist in Nashville, and as a Professor of Communications. He is the author of several books, including* The Pennsylvania Celebrities Cookbook, Straub Brewery, *and* Corresponding With History.

Richard St. Paul *is the vice chairman of the National Black Republican Association. He is also an attorney in the law firm of Patsy D. Gouldborne & Associates. In 2007, he was elected to serve on the city council in New Rochelle, New York.*

A South Florida writer specializing in nonfiction short stories, **C.A. Verno** *is a staunch Democrat. He's actively involved in local politics and has worked as a volunteer for every Democratic presidential candidate since Gary Hart, whom he first met while working as a deckhand on the yacht* Monkey Business.

Paul M. Weyrich *is chairman and CEO of the Free Congress Research and Education Foundation. He has served as president of the Kreible Institute of the Free Congress Foundation and is a founder and past director of the American Legislative Exchange Council, the founding president of the Heritage Foundation, and the current National Chairman of Coalitions for America. Mr. Weyrich is a regular guest on daily radio and television talk shows. He has published policy reports and journals and has contributed editorials to the* New York Times, *the* Washington Post, *and the* Wall Street Journal.

Copyright Information

Secret Lives of Men. Reprinted by permission of Jeff Katz. © 2008 Jeff Katz.

What a Hero Looks Like. Reprinted by permission of Dave Beckwith. © 2008 Dave Beckwith.

Tales of a Mixed Marriage. Reprinted by permission of Barbara Ann Carle. © 2008 Barbara Ann Carle.

A Blunt Instrument. Reprinted by permission of Mary Lynne Gasaway. © 2008 Mary Lynne Gasaway.

How Voting for Nixon Changed My (Love) Life. Reprinted by permission of Candace Johnson. © 2008 Candace Johnson.

Of Flags, Candles, and Friends. Reprinted by permission of Zac Byer. © 2008 Zac Byer.

The Big Switch. Reprinted by permission of Richard St. Paul. © 2008 Richard St. Paul.

The American Soldier . . . a Heritage of Heroes. Reprinted by permission of Shawn Black. © 2008 Shawn Black.

R.E.S.P.E.C.T. Reprinted by permission of Georgia A. Hubley. © 2008 Georgia A. Hubley.

The Elephant and I Remember. Reprinted by permission of Kathe Campbell. © 2008 Kathe Campbell.

Watergate: The Warm Fuzzies. Reprinted by permission of Angie Klink. © 2008 Angie Klink.

I Like Ike. Reprinted by permission of Miriam Hill. © 2008 Miriam Hill.

The Speech That Landed Barbara Bush in My Mailbox. Reprinted by permission of John E. Schlimm II. © 2008 John E. Schlimm II.

Politically Conscious Kid. Reprinted by permission of Marilyn Jensen. © 2008 Marilyn Jensen.

Confessions of a Black Conservative. Reprinted by permission of Lloyd Marcus. © 2008 Lloyd Marcus.